THE ENGLISH CIVIL WAR

Text by
PETER YOUNG
Colour plates by
MICHAEL ROFFE

First published in Great Britain in 1973 by
Osprey Publishing, Elms Court,
Chapel Way, Botley, Oxford OX2 9LP
United Kingdom
Email: *info@ospreypublishing.com*

Also published as Men-at-Arms 14 *The English Civil War*
© 1973 Osprey Publishing Ltd.

Reprinted 1977, 1979, 1981, 1982, 1983, 1984,
1985 (twice), 1987, 1988, 1989, 1990, 1992, 1994, 1998, 2000

ISBN 1 84176 040 4

Filmset in Great Britain
Printed in China through World Print Ltd.

Tourist information by Martin Marix Evans

Cartography by The Map Studio

Front cover: Sir Thomas Fairfax, later third Baron Fairfax of
Cameron (1612-71).

FOR A CATALOGUE OF ALL BOOKS PUBLISHED BY
OSPREY MILITARY, AUTOMOTIVE AND AVIATION
PLEASE WRITE TO:

The Marketing Manager, Osprey Direct USA,
PO Box 130, Sterling Heights, MI 48311-0130,
United States of America
Email: *info@OspreyDirectUSA.com*

The Marketing Manager, Osprey Direct UK,
PO Box 140, Wellingborough, Northants, NN8 4ZA,
United Kingdom.
Email: *info@OspreyDirect.co.uk*

Visit Osprey at:
www.ospreypublishing.com

Introduction

The period covered in this book begins with the outbreak of the First Civil War in 1642 and ends with the Restoration of King Charles II in 1660. Although Scots armies intervened in the struggle between King and Parliament, it is the English armies of the day which are discussed in these pages. Even though, as time went by, the Cavalier and Parliamentarian armies developed their own distinctive character, in matters of organization and uniform they differed but little, and for this reason it is not inappropriate to deal with them both in a single volume.

The general history of the war has been dealt with by such modern authorities as S. R. Gardiner, Sir Charles Firth and C. V. Wedgwood, and its

A musketeer of 1642, from the title-page of a pamphlet in the British Museum, wearing a plumed steel morion and riding-boots. He is, perhaps, a gentleman of the Honourable Artillery Company. Musketeers would normally wear shoes

military history by the late Lieutenant-Colonel A. H. Burne, D.S.O. For this reason there is no attempt here to give a detailed chronicle of the events of the war. However, a brief chronology may serve to remind readers of the main events.

Chronology

1638 & 1640

The First and Second Scots Wars.

1642

The first campaign. The King defeats the Earl of Essex at the battle of Edgehill (23 October), and, after making Oxford his capital, advances on London. He is checked at Turnham Green and goes into winter quarters.

1643

Essex takes Reading (27 April). Meanwhile, the Northern and Western Royalists, under the Earl of Newcastle and Sir Ralph Hopton respectively, gain the upper hand, though Hull and Gloucester still hold out. Prince Rupert storms Bristol (26 July) and King Charles lays siege to Gloucester (10 August), which Essex relieves (8 September). The King intercepts Essex at Newbury, but, after a severe action (20 September), draws off leaving the road to Reading and London open.

1644

The Scots Army under Lord Leven crosses the border (19 January), tipping the balance in favour of the Parliamentarians. Sir William Waller defeats the Royalists under Lord Forth at Cheriton (29 March), but is defeated by the King at Cropredy Bridge (29 June). Rupert and Newcastle are defeated by Leven, the Earl of Manchester and Lord Fairfax at Marston Moor (2 July), and, in consequence, the Cavaliers lose control of the North. King Charles surrounds Essex's Army in Cornwall and compels all but the cavalry to surrender near Fowey (2 September). At Second Newbury (27 October) the Parliamentarians concentrate forces double the King's in number, but fail to crush him. Recriminations among the Roundhead leaders brings about the formation of the New Model Army under Sir Thomas Fairfax.

1645

The New Model Army defeats the main Royalist Army at Naseby (14 June) and captures most of its foot and guns. It then worsts the Western Cavaliers under Lord Goring at Langport (10 July), who lose heart and retire gradually into Devon and Cornwall.

From this time onwards the story of the war is largely one of sieges.

1646

The New Model storms Hopton's position at Torrington (16 February). Lord Astley is compelled to surrender at Stow-on-the-Wold (21 March). The King gives himself up to the Scots before Newark (5 March). Oxford surrenders (24 June).

1647

Harlech Castle holds out until 15 March, and thereafter the Royalists have no strongholds except in the Isle of Man, the Channel Islands and the Isles of Scilly.

1648

The Second Civil War was in part an insurrection by discontented Roundhead soldiers, and in part a rising of Royalists with the support of a Scots army under the Duke of Hamilton.

Oliver Cromwell besieges Pembroke Castle and then defeats Hamilton and the Northern Royalists at Preston (17 August). Fairfax defeats the Royalists of Kent at Maidstone (1 June) and then besieges Colchester (12 June to 28 August). In Pontefract Castle a Cavalier garrison holds out until 1649.

1649

Cromwell and Henry Ireton contrive the trial of King Charles, who is beheaded on 30 January.

1649–50

Cromwell's Irish Campaign.

1650

Cromwell defeats David Leslie at the battle of Dunbar (3 September).

1651

Cromwell defeats King Charles II at the battle of Worcester (3 September).

1655

A small Royalist rising by Colonel John Penruddock in Wiltshire is quickly crushed.

1658

Death of the Protector, Oliver Cromwell, who is succeeded by his ineffective son, Richard (3 September).

1659

Sir George Booth's rising in Cheshire is crushed at the battle of Winnington Bridge.

1660

The Restoration of King Charles II is managed largely by George Monck and a strong detachment from the English garrison of Scotland (29 May).

The lives of the chief protagonists may be found in the *Dictionary of National Biography* and for this reason I have not devoted a chapter to the leaders on either side in the Civil Wars. Suffice it to say that there was a great deal of military talent and originality on either side, and that both meant

The Earl of Leven, Colonel-General Sydenham Poyntz and Colonel Edward Rossiter at the siege of Newark in 1646: a detail from Richard Clampe's contemporary plan.

Alexander Leslie, first Earl of Leven (1580?–1661), though practically illiterate, learned his trade in the Dutch and Swedish armies. He captured Edinburgh Castle for the Covenanters and won the battle of Newburn (28 August 1640) being created Earl of Leven in 1641. He led the Scots Army that invaded England in January 1644 and was in overall command of the Parliamentarian and Scottish armies that fought at Marston Moor. He did not distinguish himself on that occasion. When Goring put part of his army to flight he galloped from the field and did not draw rein until he reached Leeds. He also commanded at the sieges of York, Newcastle, Hereford and Newark.

Colonel-General Sydenham Poyntz (born 1607) was made Colonel-General of the Northern Association (27 May 1645) and Governor of York (19 August). He defeated the remnants of King Charles's horse at Rowton Heath (24 September 1645), but fell out with the Parliamentarians in 1647 and fled to Holland.

Colonel Edward Rossiter (c. 1617–69) was Major of the Lincolnshire Horse at the siege of Newark in March 1644, and later Colonel. He commanded a regiment 600 strong in the New Model and was also made Commander-in-Chief of the Parliamentarian forces in Lincolnshire. He fought at Naseby. He became M.P. for Grimsby in about 1646. On 5 July 1648 he defeated 800 Royalists at Willoughby Field although somewhat outnumbered. In the first charge he lost his helmet and was shot through the right thigh, as well as receiving some other painful wounds with a musket-ball. But he concealed his injuries and continued in command till the fight was won. Rossiter served in the Parliament of 1656. He was a Presbyterian, and had some share in bringing about the Restoration

business. As a Royalist, Captain Richard Atkyns, wrote:

'I was admitted into Prince Maurice's regiment, which was accounted the most active in the army, and most commonly placed in the out quarters; which gave me more proficiency as a soldier, in half a year's time, than generally in the Low Countries in 4 or 5 years; for there did hardly one week pass in the summer half year [1643], in which there was not a battle or skirmish fought, or beating up of quarters; . . .'

Though in theory the armies went into winter quarters there was scarcely a lull in the fighting. Wilmot took Marlborough on 5 December 1642 and Rupert stormed Cirencester on 2 February 1643. Hopton and Waller campaigned against each other in Sussex and Hampshire throughout the winter of 1643–44, and the offensive of the New Model went on throughout the last winter of the war.

This 'war without an enemy', as Waller called it, was waged with relentless zeal, and if the worst

5

excesses of the Thirty Years War were only imitated in Ireland and Scotland, England saw bloodshed enough. Counties were divided, families were split, for those who fought on either side followed their consciences. Nor are the causes for which they fought meaningless at the present day: we still have Roundheads and Cavaliers in our midst.

The Fighting

How did they fight in those days? What was a battle like? As always, tactics were governed by weapons and ground.

The English countryside in the mid-seventeenth century rather favoured the action of cavalry. Not only, of course, was there no barbed wire, but there were comparatively few enclosures of any description, and since the forests which clothed the country in the Dark and Middle Ages were already beginning to disappear, the country was, broadly speaking, suitable for movement and especially for that of large bodies of cavalry. Movement is only one element of tactics: another is fire. The important characteristics of firearms are their range, their rate of fire and the nature of the missiles they throw.

The rate of cannon-fire was very slow. The process of sponging-out and reloading was deliberate and complex. Powder was kept in small budge barrels near the guns, which were fired by the application of linstock to the touch-hole. The risk of premature explosions was very great, and it is doubtful whether it was possible to fire more than about one round every three minutes. By the time of Waterloo it was possible, using grape-shot, to get off as many as three rounds a minute

for short periods. With grape-shot the recoil was reduced and it was not necessary to run the guns up between rounds. But by 1815 all sorts of improvements had been made, with guns lightened and means of traction improved. A table of ranges will be found in the section dealing with the train.

The musket in common use was a heavy matchlock, which even a trained soldier could not hope to fire more than once a minute. Though it might kill or maim at 200 yards it was not likely to hit the target at a range of more than 50 yards. The reason for this inaccuracy was that the bullet did not fit the smooth-bore barrel at all tightly, and therefore, when propelled towards the target, it tended to wander. The disadvantages of match were all too obvious: by night it could betray the position of the musketeers, and in foul weather it simply went out.

One comes across another form of musket during this period: an early flintlock known as the 'snaphance' or 'firelock'. It was comparatively rare, and soldiers so armed were usually employed to guard the train of artillery. There was less chance of unfortunate accidents if its escort consisted of men armed with flintlocks rather than with matchlocks.

The cavalry of the period normally carried a brace of pistols and sometimes a carbine as well. These weapons were frequently used in mêlée and pursuit, but the great cavalry commanders of the Civil War soon came to rely chiefly on the sword. This is true both of Cromwell and of Rupert.

However, if the cavalry, Cavalier and Roundhead alike, came to rely upon shock action they could resort to firearms if they chose. Similarly, though the bayonet had not yet been introduced, the musketeers could join in a mêlée with their swords or, better still, the sharp-pointed butts of their heavy muskets. But the pikemen, who made up at least one-third of the infantry were condemned to shock action and nothing more. They were far from mobile, having to move in close formation in order to form their hedgehog, and being weighed down with helmet and corselet.

It is not very safe to generalize about the battles of the Civil Wars, for the tactics were far from stereotyped. But usually, and at least in the bigger

Sir Thomas Fairfax, later third Baron Fairfax of Cameron (1612–71), served at the siege of Bois-le-Duc (1629) and in the First Scots War. From 1642 to 1646 he was the life and soul of his father's small force which kept up the unequal struggle with Newcastle's Northern Army until it was destroyed at Marston Moor. His tactical skill and gallant leadership as well as his victories at Wakefield (21 May 1643), and Nantwich (25 January 1644) led to his selection as commander of the New Model Army, whose victories at Naseby, Langport, Torrington and elsewhere put an end to the First Civil War. Fairfax, a taciturn man, was no politician, and power gradually passed to his second-in-command, Oliver Cromwell. His wife's sympathies were Royalist and he played no part in the trial of Charles I

Prince Rupert (1619–82). The portrait below is from an original by Sir Anthony van Dyck, and that on the left by Gerard von Honthorst. With the possible exceptions of the Marquis of Montrose and Lord Hopton, Prince Rupert was the outstanding Royalist leader of his day. Unfortunately his victories at Powick Bridge, Cirencester, Lichfield Close, Chalgrove Field, Bristol and Newark were cancelled out by the disaster at Marston Moor which lost the North for the King. He was better as the commander of a small mobile army, a 'brigade group', than of a big army. This may be attributed to his youth. He was a thoroughly scientific soldier, as much at home in a siege as a cavalry charge, and interested in the development of weapons. In later life he proved a bold and efficient admiral

battles, it was customary to draw up an army with the foot and guns in the centre, and the cavalry on the wings. Dragoons, if present, were mostly placed on the outer wings of the cavalry. The smaller guns – often called 'drakes' – were placed in pairs with the brigades of foot, while the bigger pieces were planted further back.

There was usually a reserve, often consisting of both horse and foot. The commander, on horseback, was often to be found at the head of the reserve, but it was not the fashion to set up a command post at some building or upon some eminence. It cannot have been easy for gallopers to deliver their messages. Prince Rupert's great standard, taken at Marston Moor, may have been intended to mark his headquarters. In the rear of the army, occasionally formed into a wagon-laager, was the baggage-train.

Battles sometimes began with the commander parading down his line exhorting his men, or giving them tactical instructions, as King Charles and Prince Rupert did at Edgehill. Sometimes, as at Braddock Down, the Royalists had prayers, or the Roundheads, as before Powick Bridge, sang a psalm. Then came the preliminary bombardment which was not generally very effective. Exceptions are Braddock Down where a surprise burst of fire from the two small Royalist guns struck terror into the Roundheads; Hopton Heath where 'Roaring Meg' caused heavy casualties among Sir John Gell's Roundhead stand of pikes; and Langport where the artillery of the New Model quickly silenced Goring's big guns.

The next phase was usually a general advance, sometimes heralded by some preliminary skirmishing by the dragoons. Usually it was the cavalry that came to grips, before the foot came to push of pike. The victor was usually the one who could dispose of his opponent's horse, and having done so could turn upon the as yet unbroken foot of his enemy's army. This was the case both at Marston Moor and at Naseby.

The last phase was the pursuit, or 'execution' as it was called. Often more fell in flight than in the actual battle, and the victor made a good haul of prisoners, especially from among the foot.

Some of the so-called battles were very small, involving not more than a few thousand on each side. In the biggest, Marston Moor, there may

have been 50,000 men engaged but they were from five different armies, those of Rupert and Newcastle (Royalist), of Leven, Manchester and Fairfax (Scots and Parliamentarian).

The control of a battle was not simple. General officers very often led charges and fought hand-to-hand. Men like Sir Thomas Fairfax and Prince Rupert were never content to sit on their horses upon some lofty eminence, whilst their men fought it out, and Rupert, indeed, had his own technique of running a cavalry fight which called for his personal leadership. Sir Edward Southcote, when describing the Prince's way of fighting, says, 'he had a select body of horse who always attended him, and in every attack they received the enemy's shot without returning it; but one and all bore with all their force upon the adversaries till they broke their ranks, and charged quite through them: then they rallied, and when they [the Roundheads] were in disorder, fell upon their rear, and slaughtered them with scarce any opposition'. The select body no doubt was the Lifeguard under Sir Richard Crane, and Prince Rupert's Regiment of Horse, which even as late as Naseby could muster 400 men.

A mêlée could be a difficult and dangerous affair if the enemy stood to their work. At Roundway Down Colonel Sir John Byron describes how, echoing Rupert's orders at Edgehill, he commanded that:

'not a man should discharge his pistol till the enemy had spent all his shot, which was punctually observed, so that first they gave us a volley

The Dunbar Medal is thought to have been the first given to all ranks of a victorious English army. The obverse shows a portrait of Oliver Cromwell and the words THE LORD OF HOSTS, which was the 'field word' or password at the battle. The reverse shows the House of Commons in session

George Monck, first Duke of Albemarle, K.G. (1608–70), a Devon man, was one of the most distinguished professional soldiers of his day. He was in the Cadiz expedition of 1625 and distinguished himself at the famous siege of Breda in 1637, in which so many of the leaders of our Civil Wars took part. Captured at Nantwich in 1644 he was sent to the Tower, where he wrote his *Observations upon Military and Political Affairs*, which are full of good sense. After the beheading of Charles I he joined Cromwell, and a regiment was formed for him which is now the Coldstream Guards. He fought at Dunbar and was afterwards Commander-in-Chief in Scotland. He was chiefly responsible for the restoration of King Charles II

of their carbines, then of their pistols, and then we fell in with them, and gave them ours in their teeth, yet they would not quit their ground, but stood pushing for it a pretty space, till it pleased God (I thinke) to put new spirit into our tired horse as well as into our men, so that though it were up the hill, and that a steep one, we over-bore them, and with that violence, that we forced them to fall foul upon other reserves of horse that stood behind to second them, & so swept their whole body of horse out of the field, and left their foot naked, and pursued them near 3 miles, over the downs in Bristol way till they came to a precipice, where their fear made them so valiant that they galloped as if it had been plain ground, and many of them brake both their own and their horses' necks.'

This is a spirited account by one whose regiment was the oldest in the King's Army, one like those described by a Roundhead eyewitness of Marston Moor who wrote: 'The enemy's horse . . . stood very firm a long while, coming to a close fight with the sword, and standing like an iron-wall, so that they were not easily broken. . . .'

The heavy cavalry of those days, unless skilfully handled, could easily rout those of their own side. Hopton gives a marvellously vivid account of the 'ruffe medly' at Babylon Hill at the very beginning of the war (7 September 1642). The Roundheads nearly took him by surprise by marching out of Yeovil 'by a secret way they had made over the fields'. He had four troops of horse; and he sent two into the attack, supported by a third, keeping the fourth in reserve. Captain Edward Stowell:

'charg'd verie gallantly and routed the enemy, but withall (his troops consisting of new horse, and the Enemy being more in number) was rowted himselfe; and Capt. [Henry] Moreton,[1] being a little too neere him, was likewise broaken with the same shocke, and the trueth is in verie short tyme, all the horse on both sides were in a confusion: At the same tyme a troope of the Enemyes horse charg'd up in the hollow-way on the right hand, where ([Colonel] Sir Tho: Lunsford having forgotten to put a party of muskettiers as before) they found noe opposicion till they came among the voluntiers [Stowell's troop] upon the topp of the Hill, where by a very extraordinary accident, Sir James Colborne with a fowling gunne shott at the Captain[2] in the head of the troope, and at the same instant Mr. John Stowell charg'd him single (by which of their hands it was, it is not certaine) but the Captain was slayne, and the troope (being rawe fellowes) immedyately rowted. In this extreame confusion Sir Ralph Hopton was enforced to make good [cover] the retreate with a few officers and Gentlemen that rallyed to him. . . .'

Sending off his foot he withdrew to Sherborne Castle with little loss.

Naturally not all charges were cavalry against cavalry: sometimes it was a question of horse against foot, and this had peculiar hazards since the latter would take cover behind hedges and walls.

Byron whose horse had been shot in the throat with a musket-ball describes the fighting in which Lord Falkland fell at First Newbury:

'The passage being then made somewhat wide, and I not having another horse, drew in my own troop first, giving orders for the rest to

Colonel John Russell, M.P. (1620–87) was General of the Horse in Essex's Army. As Lieutenant-Colonel of Lord Wentworth's Regiment of Dragoons he fought at the storming of Cirencester (2 February 1643) and at Chalgrove Field (18 June 1643). He was wounded at the storming of Bolton on 28 May 1644, was at the storming of Leicester (30 May 1645), and was wounded at Naseby. He was in the defence of Bristol in 1645

follow and charged the enemy, who entertained us with a great salvo of musket shot, and discharged their two drakes upon us laden with case shot, which killed some and hurt many of my men, so that we were forced to wheel off and could not meet them at that charge.'

The dogged Byron was not the man to be put off. He rallied his men, and while he did so the Roundheads pulled back their drakes. Another charge beat them back to the end of the close, 'where they faced us again, having the advantage of a hedge at their backs and poured in another volley of shot upon us, when [Colonel] Sir Thomas Aston's horse was killed under him, and withal kept us off with their pikes'. The battlefield of Newbury was full of enclosures in those days: no place for horse.

Little Dean (11 April 1643), it seems, was not much better. Captain Richard Atkyns of Prince

Cromwell. Both portraits are by Samuel Cooper, the one on the left from an unfinished miniature. The signature is as Protector in 1657, and the second Great Seal of the Protector is of 1655

Maurice's Regiment had one of his several narrow escapes that day:

'The charge was seemingly as desperate as any I was ever in; it being to beat the enemy from a wall which was a strong breastwork, with a gate in the middle; possessed by above 200 musketeers, besides horse: we were to charge down a steep plain hill, of above 12 score yards[3] in length; as good a mark as they could wish: our party consisting of between two and three hundred horse, not a man of them would follow us, so the officers, about 10 or 12[4] of us, agreed to gallop down in as good order as we could, and make a desperate charge upon them; the enemy seeing our resolutions, never fired at us at all, but run away; and we (like young soldiers) after them, doing execution upon them; but one Captain Hanmer being better horsed than myself, in pursuit, fell upon their ambuscade and was killed horse and man: I had only time enough to turn my horse and run for my life. This party of ours, that would not be drawn on at first, by this time, seeing our success; came into the town after us, and stopped our retreat; and finding that we were pursued by the enemy, the horse in the front, fell back upon the rear, and they were so wedged together, that they routed themselves, so as there was no passage for a long time: all this while the enemy were upon me, Cutting my [buff] coat upon my armour in several places, and discharging pistols as they got up to me, being the outermost man; which Major [Thomas] Sheldon declared to my very great advantage: ... [Major Leighton,[5] came up and] made good a stone house, and so prepared for them with musketeers; that one volley of shot made them retreat: they were so near me, that a musket bullet from one of our men took off one of the bars of my [steel] cap I charged with, and went through my hair and did me no hurt.'

Many and varied were the adventures that might befall a cavalryman as he tried to get the better of some opponent in the 'Balaclava mêlée' of those days. Like Sir Richard Bulstrode, he could be wounded while pursuing an enemy at Edgehill, and, obviously striving like any sensible horse-soldier to attack on the left or bridle-hand side, be wounded by a vicious swing of the pole-axe! Bulstrode was saved by his colonel, Sir Thomas Byron, who pistolled the Roundhead. The episode at Newark (21 March 1644), when a Parliamentarian trooper laid his hand on Prince Rupert's collar only to have it sliced off by Sir William Neale, serves to show that the cavalry fights of those days were not a battle of flowers.

As for the foot, it was their business to advance steadily in rank and file until they came to push of pike. Sometimes, as at Braddock Down, one side would not await the shock; or, as at Stratton, they counter-attacked; or sometimes, as in the case of Edgehill, finding they could make no impression, 'each as if by mutuall consent retired some few paces, and they stuck down their colours, continuing to fire at one another even till night; a thing so very extraordinary, that nothing less than so many witnesses as were there present could make it credible' – *King James II*. These young soldiers, Roundhead and Cavalier alike, who fought it out at Edgehill, were not unworthy ancestors of the 'Thin Red Line' or the superb infantry of 1914, for the one virtue that the foot-soldier needs above all, then and now, is tenacity.

The Horse

As a general rule regiments of horse were 500 strong and were organized in six troops, each some 70 strong. In practice, however, strengths varied considerably, especially in the Royalist armies, and this was the case from the very outset. The raising of horse presented peculiar difficulties. It was not easy to find officers who had both tactical skill and a knowledge of animal management. In some parts of the country it was not possible to obtain large numbers of horses. The

Charles Gerard, first Baron Gerard of Brandon and Earl of Macclesfield (d. 1694). Gerard was a captain in the Dutch service and then in the Scots War. He commanded a tertia of foot, in which his regiment of bluecoats served, at the battle of Edgehill. He was a gallant soldier and was wounded several times, besides distinguishing himself at First Newbury, Newark and elsewhere. He was a firm friend of Prince Rupert who got him the command in South Wales, where he proved very unpopular with the local gentry. Gerard was with Turenne at the siege of Arras in 1654, and commanded Charles II's Lifeguard of Horse in 1660. In later years he supported Monmouth, though he did not take part in his rebellion. He lived to command William III's bodyguard in 1688. His portrait by Dobson is in the Dunedin Public Art Gallery in New Zealand

Cornish Army, which Hopton led at Stratton and Lansdown, was seriously short of cavalry until it joined hands with the Marquis of Hertford and Prince Maurice at Chard on 4 June 1643.

	HORSE	DRAGOONS	FOOT	FIELD-PIECES
Hopton	500	300	3,000	4–5
Hertford and Maurice	1,500	—	1,000	10–11
	2,000	300	4,000	14–16

At the rendezvous at Aldbourne on 10 April 1644 four of the Royalist regiments were 300 strong and had each, seven or eight troops. These powerful units were the regiments of the Earl of Forth, Prince Maurice, Lord Percy and Colonel

Thomas Howard. At the other end of the scale there were Colonels Sir Allen Apsley and George Gunter, who had only one troop apiece; and Sir George Vaughan who had eighty men organized in two troops.

At a muster of the Parliamentarian Army at Tiverton in the summer of 1644, under the Earl of Essex, there were seven regiments present. They, too, varied very much in size and composition.

COLONEL	TROOPS	OFFICERS	MEN
Sir Philip Stapleton	8	86	639
Sir William Balfour	6	62	432
Hans Behre	5	54	371
John Dalbier	4	43	267
James Sheffield	6	61	414
Sir Robert Pye	3	32	208
Edmond Harvey	6	72	389
	38	410	2,720

In addition there was Captain Abercromby's company of dragoons, consisting of nine officers and sixty-five dragoons. At first sight the large number of officers may seem surprising, but in those days non-commissioned officers and even trumpeters were included under that head.

The composition of the normal troop was:

Field officer or captain	1
Captain-lieutenant or lieutenant	1
Cornet	1
Quartermaster	1
Corporals	3
Trumpeters	2
Saddler	1
Farrier	1
Troopers	60
	71

In the Royalist armies regiments usually had three field officers: colonel, lieutenant-colonel and major. In the Parliamentarian armies only exceptionally strong regiments, such as Cromwell's famous unit, which was twice the usual size, had lieutenant-colonels. The quartermasters were commissioned officers. I have never come across any individual Royalist soldier with the appointment of farrier or saddler, but they cannot very

'The Poulett Family Return from the Wars.' This charming if somewhat primitive picture is especially revealing about the horses. These heavy, handsome beasts were exactly what the cavalryman of those days wanted for a charger. Note, too, the elaborately built-up saddles.

The older Cavalier in this group is John, first Baron Poulett (1586–1649) of Hinton St George, Somerset, who was raised to the peerage in 1627. He served in the West Country, as did his sons Sir John (1615–65), the second baron, and Amias

well have done without them. In the organization of Essex's 1642 Army they are specifically mentioned.

FORMATIONS

The cavalry of the Civil Wars seem to have used rather deeper or heavier formations than those of more modern times. Bulstrode tells us that at Edgehill the Royalist horse were three deep, while the Parliamentarians occasionally, as at Newark (21 March 1644), doubled their files and charged six deep. The picture that Cruso gives (Plate G) cannot, therefore, have been very far from the reality, though Rupert and Cromwell relied on the sword rather than the pistol. The latter, describing the action at Grantham, speaks of advancing at 'a pretty round trot'.

Rupert one imagines favoured a faster pace, and the Earl of Northampton's first attack at Hopton Heath (19 March 1643) was described by a Roundhead eyewitness as 'a very fierce charge, French-like', an interesting comment, for Condé's great victory at Rocroi was fought that very year and the French owed a great deal of their success to the dash of their cavalry. At Powick Bridge (23 September 1642) Sir Lewis Dyve's troop, which was in Rupert's Regiment, received the Roundhead charge at the halt, firing a volley of carbine and pistol shot. They were roughly handled and when, a month later, they fought at Edgehill they received specific orders to 'march as close as was possible, keeping their Ranks with Sword in Hand, to receive the Enemy's shot, without firing either Carbin or Pistol, till we broke in amongst the Enemy, and then to make use of our Fire-Arms as need should require; which Order was punctually observed' – *Sir Richard Bulstrode*.

Discipline

The Cavalier, Sir Philip Warwick, records the conversation of a sober friend of his with an acquaintance serving under Sir Thomas Fairfax. The Roundhead boasted of the sanctity of their army and the negligence of the Cavaliers. 'Faith,' retorted the Royalist, 'thou sayest true; for in our army we have the Sins of men (drinking and wenching) but in yours you have those of devils, spiritual pride and rebellion'.

At the beginning of the war they had a good many other sins as well. In 1642 Essex and his senior officers were hampered in their attempts to impose discipline. For one thing many of them were 'pluralists' and could not be in two places at once. Many of the colonels of foot were members of one of the Houses of Parliament and also commanders of troops of horse. But a more serious factor working against good order was the feeling pervading the Roundhead Army that, high or low, they were all rebels together.

An intelligent Londoner, a sergeant in Denzil Holles's Regiment, wrote letters to his master, which paint a lurid picture of the army's discipline, while Brian Twyne has recorded some of their disorders at Oxford. We find instances of kirk-rapine, poaching deer, murderous and drunken brawling on a large scale, mutiny; plundering of fellow soldiers as well as papists and malignants. It was recorded that many soldiers flung away their arms and deserted.

In September Hampden and five other colonels complained that their soldiers plundered every-where, 'The truth is unless we were able to execute some exemplary punishment upon the principle malefactors, we have no hope to redress this horrid enormity.' They were rightly afraid that, 'if this go on awhile, the army will grow as odious to the country as the Cavaliers'. Lord Brooke and Lord Saye and Sele both made some attempt to assert discipline, the latter even sending some mutineers to prison. But it was not until 9 November that Parliament eventually laid down *The Laws and Ordinances of War established for the better conduct of the Army*.

It is an odd fact that, except for the mutineers imprisoned by Lord Saye and Sele at Oxford, the only instance of punishment in Essex's Army that Sergeant Wharton records was when, on 27 August, some soldiers at Coventry took the law into their own hands and ill-treated a whore, who had followed them from London. She 'was taken by the soldiers, and first led about the city, then set in the pillory, after in the cage, then duckt in a river, and at the last banisht the City'.

Pillaging and desertion were not readily checked by *The Laws and Ordinances*, partly because the soldiers had too long been allowed to do as they pleased. Cromwell, though he had a taste for iconoclasm as he showed at Peterborough Cathedral (22 April 1643), drew the line at pillage and marauding. As early as May 1643 *Speciall Passages* records that,

'no man swears but he pays his twelve pence; if he be drunk he is set in the stocks, or worse, if one calls the other "Roundhead" he is cashiered; insomuch that the countries where they come leap for joy of them, and come in and join with them. How happy were it if all the forces were thus disciplined.'

But, of course, they were not. As late as Adwalton Moor (29 June 1643) Sir Thomas Fairfax tells us that the Northern Forces did not yet have martial law among them, and it was left to Almighty Providence to punish four malefactors who were plundering the corpse of the Royalist Colonel George Heron. Fairfax records with satisfaction their death from a cannon-shot. As early as April 1643 Cromwell had two deserters whipped in the market-place at Huntingdon and 'turned off as renegadoes'.

A standard of the Civil Wars, from a sketch by W. Y. Carman, said to have belonged to a Royalist called Colonel Rice Yate. There does not appear to have been a colonel of that name – perhaps his descendants promoted him. Nor does the motto look like a Royalist one. Perhaps, indeed, the standard was a trophy rather than that belonging to a troop of Cavaliers

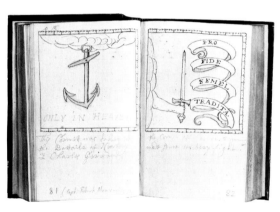

Two Parliamentarian cavalry standards. These are taken from a book of colours preserved in the National Army Museum, Captain Robert Manwaring evidently lost his cornet in the charges by which Charles Gerard's brigade of horse swept the Roundhead right from the field at the first battle of Newbury, and had another cornet made. According to the law of arms he should have done so only if one of his troop had taken a standard from the enemy in the meanwhile

Sir William Waller was another Parliamentarian who strove to enforce discipline. Some court-martial papers have survived which date back to 1644. Mutiny and mass desertion seriously reduced his army after his defeat at Cropredy Bridge (29 June), and it is of great interest to see what his disciplinary troubles were, and what was done about them. A 'Councell of Warr' at Phemham (Farnham ?) on 22 April ordered that 'the (Provost) Marshall Generall', whenever he found a private soldier drunk, 'shall have power to inflict the punishment of puttinge on a paire of handcuffs, and with a chaine to drawe the party up untill hee stand on tipptoe with a kan or jugg about his necke neere the maine Guard, and there to stand according to discrecon'. As a punishment it sounds rather more severe than that of the stocks, which Cromwell had employed for the same offence the previous year. This punishment was also given to Phillip Warnington who had abused and cut a fellow soldier (17 July); in addition he was cashiered.

Robert Devereux, third Earl of Essex (1591–1646) commanded the main Parliamentarian Army from 1642 to 1644. He had served as a colonel in the Dutch Army and had been vice-admiral in the Cadiz expedition of 1625. He was no great strategist or disciplinarian, nor was he particularly energetic. But he was a man of courage. His chief exploit was his relief of Gloucester in September 1643

The same court ordered that one John Boreman for 'Running away from his Cullors severall tymes', was 'to be hang'd by the neck untill hee be dead'. This seems to have been the ordinary punishment for desertion, though the court was sometimes more merciful; as in the case of two men who confessed to robbing a tailor at Woodstock of a doublet and a pattern for a pair of breeches who were ordered to 'lye neck and Heels together one whole day and be fead with no other food then bread and water, and then set at Liberty'. The same court ordered that Henry Stone who had confessed to 'plundering a shirt, an apron and some other triviall things, shall have the Gatlopp once through the whole Regiment and be ignominiously discharged the Army'. The *Gantelope* or 'running the gauntlet' was common in the Swedish and German armies. The men formed a lane facing inwards and the prisoner passed

down it, his speed checked by a sergeant with his halbert. Each man was allowed one blow at the criminal with a switch or with his ramrod.

A Major Willett was cashiered (11 October 1644) for presenting a false muster, that is, attempting to draw pay for men who did not exist. On 17 October Corporal Read was cashiered for robbery, with the added indignity that his sword was to be broken over his head.

The Roundhead committee which ran the garrison of Stafford (1643–45) took it upon itself to impose a high standard of discipline. On 11 December 1643 it was ordered that Lieutenant Yong should 'forthwith be casheered out of the Towne' for being drunk, neglecting his guard, letting down the drawbridge at the 'Geolegate' at 10 o'clock at night and going to the further end of the foregate. He was to stand in the market-place 'with a paper in his hat upon the market-day wherein shall be wrote his offence'.

'18 March, 1644

'Ordered that the Gunner which did committ fornication shall bee set upon the greate gun with a marke uppon his backe through the Garrison and then disgracefully expulsed.

'27 March 1644

'Lieutenant Dutton for plundering and for terrorizing the inhabitants of the county was to "be committed to prison and by the next conveniency sent to the Parliament to receive punishment according to theyr ordinance in the case".'

It would be idle to pretend that the Royalist armies did not suffer in like manner from disciplinary troubles. Plundering and desertion seem to have been the crimes most prevalent, and, since the King was unable to keep his men constantly paid, it is not surprising that they either tried to subsist by marauding, or just went home. It would be unwise indeed to assert that the Cavaliers were better disciplined than the Roundheads, though in 1642 – while the pay lasted – it may be true, at least of the infantry. The truth, is that both sides had such severe administrative difficulties that neither army was blameless, and so the unfortunate country people who had to find them quarters suffered the consequences.

In the autumn of 1642, at the outset of the war, according to Clarendon who was not one to praise

The Queen's Sconce at Newark. This work was built to cover the bridge where the Fosse Way crosses the River Devon. It stands on a slightly elevated spur of gravel and has a good view of the flat meadows north and west of the town. It covers a little more than three acres, and is surrounded by a ditch up to 70 feet wide, and 12 to 15 feet deep. The fort was almost certainly surrounded by a palisade. This may have been in the bottom of the ditch where it could not be hit by cannon-balls. In 1957 Newark Corporation cleared the fort of a dense jungle of bushes and brambles, so that it is now possible to see its original outline. (Courtesy of the Royal Commission on Historial Monuments (England), Crown Copyright)

military men, the Royalist army 'either by the care and diligence of the officers, or by the good inclinations and temper of the soldiers themselves' was 'in so good order and discipline, that, during the King's stay at Shrewsbury, there was not a disorder of name, the country being kind to the soldiers, and the soldiers just and regardful to the country'. Free loans and contributions from the gentry and substantial inhabitants, and the noblemen with the army, guaranteed the pay of the men so that they had no cause for discontent.

Mrs Hutchinson speaks of Sir Lewis Dyve's troop at Nottingham as 'plundering all the honest men of their arms', but to disarm rebels can scarcely be so stigmatized. At Birmingham, a very hostile place, the King actually had two men executed for stealing from the house of a Roundhead soldier.

Certainly, without question, Royalist troopers occupied themselves with plundering Essex's baggage-train in Kineton during the battle of Edgehill – though one Roundhead captain accuses dragoons of his own side of this! As early as November 1642 Sir John Byron's men did a great deal of malicious damage at the house of the Roundhead, Bulstrode Whitelocke.

The manner of framing a Quadrangle Skonfe.

THis Foure-fquare Skonfe, is of greater ftrength than your Triangle, and if it be favoured with a ftrong Scituation, as great Rivers, or upon a Rocke, or where it may be flankered from the Bulworks of a Fort, it will ftand in great ftead ; otherwife it is not to be taken for a ftrength of any moment . The Bulworkes and Curtines are to be made very high, thicke, and ftrong, that it may endure the battering of the Enemies Ordnance.

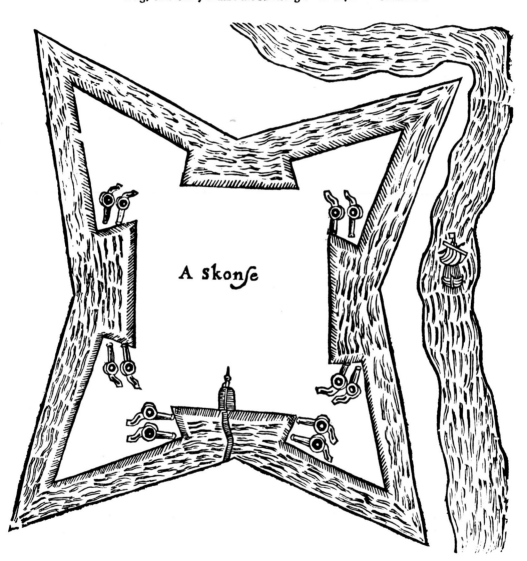

A skonfe

A plan of a sconce, from an illustration in Robert Ward's *Animadversions of Warre*, 1639; a sconce was a detached fort with bastions. (Courtesy of the Royal Commission on Historical Monuments (England), Crown Copyright)

20

A Royalist troop on the march, from the monument of Sir Richard Astley, Bart., at Patshull. Further particulars of Astley and his troop will be found in the description of Plate C, which is reconstructed in part from the trumpeters shown here

As the war went on the Royalists strove to uphold discipline with the gallows and the wooden horse. The lash was not very much used though a soldier who had ravished two women was tied to a tree, with his shoulders and chest naked, so Richard Symonds of the Lifeguard of Horse tells us, 'and every carter of the trayne and carriages was to have a lash'. He tells us that this was a Spanish punishment.

It may be that the King was not sufficiently severe in his discipline. But at Wing on 28 August 1645 he did have a soldier hanged for stealing the communion plate. Nicholas writes to Rupert from Oxford (11 May 1643) 'Sir James Mills was lately shot by an officer upon a private quarrel; and the last night Lieutenant Cranefeild was wounded by one Captain Hastings upon the like occasion. There is here no punishment, and therefore nothing but disorder can be expected.'

Perhaps this very complaint led to a tightening of discipline. Certainly Colonel Sir Nicholas Crispe, who killed Sir James Enyan in a duel which he had not provoked, had to answer for it to a court martial. Colonel Richard Feilding lost his regiment – and very nearly his life – for surrendering Reading. Sir Richard Cave was court-martialled for surrendering Hereford, but was acquitted.

Colonel Henry Windebank was shot (3 May 1645) for surrendering Bletchingdon House to Cromwell, and Rupert himself was dismissed for the surrender of Bristol (10 September 1645); and, although he was eventually acquitted, he never fully recovered his position in his uncle's favour.

The Rupert Correspondence contains many letters in which Royalist commanders complain about plundering. This shows at least that the senior officers, with a few notable exceptions, intended to keep their men in order. In this some were more successful than others, and this may, of course, be said of both sides. If pay, or at least

15. *Recover your Pistoll.*   **16.** *Present and giue Fire.*

23   **24** *The marching Postúres of ý Harquebusiers*

Cuirassiers and Harquebusiers, from John Cruso's *Militarie Instructions for the Cavall'rie* (1632).

Sir Arthur Hesilrige's 'Lobsters' were probably armed very much like the trooper with the pistol, though it is probable that during the Civil Wars cuirassiers wore the triple-barred lobster-tailed helmet rather than a close helmet.

The common type of cavalryman of 1642 was called a 'harquebusier', but by that time the harquebus seems to have disappeared. Back and breastplate, pot helmet and perhaps a left arm guard, seem to have been the armour generally in vogue; with a sword and a pair of pistols for armament. That some cavalrymen had fowling-pieces or carbines is certain, but they seem to have been the exception rather than the rule. Cruso's harquebusier seems to be wearing a kind of burgonet. It must be remembered that his book saw the light ten years before Edgehill, but the triple-barred helmet must have been the most common 'pot' among both Cavalier and Roundhead troopers, and there is evidence that morions of the sort worn in 1588 were to be seen in the Civil Wars. There is no reason why a helmet fifty-four years old should not be serviceable. Note the cruel bits and spurs that these troopers use; they rode with the brakes on and the choke out!

rations, cannot be assured, marauding is bound to follow and discipline can no longer be maintained. This is a truth as old as war itself.

The Foot

In theory a regiment was 1,300 strong and was organized in ten companies. The field officers, colonel, lieutenant-colonel and major had companies, which numbered 200, 160 and 140 respectively. Each of the seven captains had a company of 100 men. Very often the colonel was also a general officer or the governor of some fortress; frequently the lieutenant-colonel or even the major was the real commanding officer. In addition, one of the field officers was sometimes taken away to act as brigade-major of the formation in which the regiment was serving. The duties which in modern times are carried out by the adjutant and the R.S.M. were then performed by the major. I have found no adjutant in an English army before 1665, and no 'sergeant-major' in the modern sense of R.S.M., before about 1720. In 1642 the term 'sergeant-major' was still frequently used for the major, that is, the third senior officer of a regiment.

The staff of a regiment usually included a quartermaster, a chaplain, a provost-marshal (in the Parliamentarian Army), a surgeon and his mate, a carriage-master and a drum-major. In Royalist regiments one occasionally finds the wagoner or wagon-master signing for stores, instead of the quartermaster.

The organization of a normal company was:

Captain	1
Lieutenant	1
Ensign	1
Gentleman-of-the-arms	1
Sergeants	2
Corporals	3
Drummers	2
Soldiers	100

The colonel had a captain-lieutenant instead of a lieutenant. This officer does not seem to have been paid extra for commanding the colonel's company, but at least he ranked above the other lieutenants and was next in line for a company, should there be a casualty. Each company had a colour which was carried by the ensign.

The gentleman-of-the-arms seems to have been a Royalist innovation. It was much more difficult for them to obtain arms than it was for the Parliamentarians, and therefore it behoved them to take good care of those they had, especially the firearms. This officer seems to have been a kind of company armourer sergeant.

Both pikemen and musketeers were to be found in each company, the theoretical proportion being one pikeman to every two musketeers. There is some evidence, however, that the Royalists at Edgehill had as many pikemen as musketeers, and from a tactical point of view that may have been an advantage.

Throughout the war regiments varied very much in numbers. In 1642 many were up to strength, but battle casualties, sickness and desertion soon took their toll. Neither did every regiment have its ten companies: on the Royalist side eight seems to have been a more usual number.

This table illustrates the wastage in the Royalist infantry. The figures for November 1642 are calculated from a pay warrant; those for April 1644 were taken from a muster of the garrison of Reading.

COLONEL	Nov. 1642
John Belasyse	505
Sir William Pennyman	685
Richard Feilding	460
Richard Bolle	560
Sir Edward Fitton	460
Sir Edward Stradling	715
Sir Thomas Salusbury	910

COLONEL	April 1644
Sir Theophilus Gilby	355

Sir James Pennyman	479
Sir Jacob Astley	217
George Lisle	270
Anthony Thelwall	196
John Stradling	351
Sir Charles Lloyd	409

It will be noticed that not one of these seven regiments still had its original colonel.

At Edgehill the Royalist foot, some 10,000 strong, was organized in five tertias or brigades. At Naseby, where the foot were certainly not more than 4,000 strong, there were only three brigades. At Edgehill four of the brigades each had three regiments, while one had five. By 1644 tertias had as many as nine weak regiments in them.

In 1642 the regiments of the King's main army came from many different parts of the kingdom. They included:

COLONEL/REGIMENT

Charles Gerard	Lancashire
	Cheshire
	North Wales
Sir Ralph Dutton	Gloucestershire
John Belasyse	Yorkshire
	Nottinghamshire
Richard Feilding	Partly from Herefordshire
Sir Thomas Lunsford	Somerset
Richard Bolle	Staffordshire
Sir Edward Fitton	Cheshire
Sir Edward Stradling	South Wales, especially Glamorgan
The King's Lifeguard	Lincolnshire
	Derbyshire
	Cheshire
Lord General	Lincolnshire
Sir John Beaumont	Staffordshire
Sir Gilbert Gerard	Lancashire
Sir Thomas Salusbury	North Wales, especially Denbighshire and Flint
Lord Molyneux	Lancashire
Earl of Northampton	North Oxfordshire
	Warwickshire

Sir Lewis Dyve and Thomas Blagge, who came from the Roundhead counties of Bedfordshire and Suffolk, were probably not able to raise many men in those parts. Dyve seems to have got at least two companies from Lincolnshire.

As time went by the King's main army drew many of its recruits from Wales, though it was reinforced by several Northern regiments in 1643. Two of these arrived in May with a convoy of ammunition, while several others reached Oxford with the Queen in July. On the whole, the Northern Royalists went into the army raised by the Earl of Newcastle – the army which was virtually destroyed at Marston Moor. The Cornish, who were as warlike as they were loyal, defended their territory with their trained bands, but as these would not go 'abroad', five 'voluntary' regiments were raised. These volunteers made the nucleus of Hopton's Western Army which, after his victory at Stratton, joined Prince Maurice in the Lansdown-Roundway Down campaign and paved the way for Prince Rupert's capture of Bristol; like Newcastle's Whitecoats, they were very good foot.

So far as one can tell the Earl of Essex's Army, which was the main Roundhead army, was recruited in London, the south Midlands and the Home Counties.

COLONEL	COUNTY
Earl of Essex	Essex
Sir John Merrick	London
(1) Lord Saye and Sele (2) Sir John Meldrum	North Oxfordshire
Lord Brooke	Warwickshire
Denzil Holles, M.P.	London
Thomas Ballard	Buckinghamshire
John Hampden, M.P.	Buckinghamshire

In the matter of wastage, Parliamentarian regiments fared worse than those of the King, and some did not survive even the first campaign. Lord Wharton's and Lord Mandeville's, which, among others, fled at Edgehill, were disbanded in the following month. Denzil Holles's Regiment fought bravely at Edgehill, but was cut to pieces at Brentford and did not survive the disaster. On 1 October 1642, Sir Henry Cholmley's 1,200-strong Regiment fled at Edgehill and was evidently punished for its pains, since only 552 men remained on 23 November. Lord Brooke, who had about 1,000 men when he entered Oxford at the end of September, had but 480 in mid-November. Thomas Ballard mustered 808 officers and men on 17 October 1642 but only had 439, not counting officers, on 11 November. Some of his companies were very thin by that time.

1 King Charles I (1600–49) in 1644
2 Sir Edward Walker (1612–77)
3 Prince Charles, later King Charles II
  (1630–85) in 1642

MICHAEL ROFFE

A

Sir Charles Lucas (k. 1648)

B

Trumpeter,
Captain Sir Richard Astley's
Troop of Horse

MICHAEL ROFFE

C

Officer of Horse or Dragoons

D

1 Pikeman, Lord Brooke's Regiment
2 Roundhead Commander
3 Musketeer

MICHAEL ROFFE

E

1 Lieutenant of a bluecoat regiment
2 Colonel Nathaniel Fiennes (1608?–69)
3 Colonel Sir Richard Willys (1614–90)

F

1 Ensign, Lamplugh's Regiment of Foot
2 Drummer of a redcoat regiment
3 Royalist Sergeant of a green-
  coat regiment

MICHAEL ROFFE

G

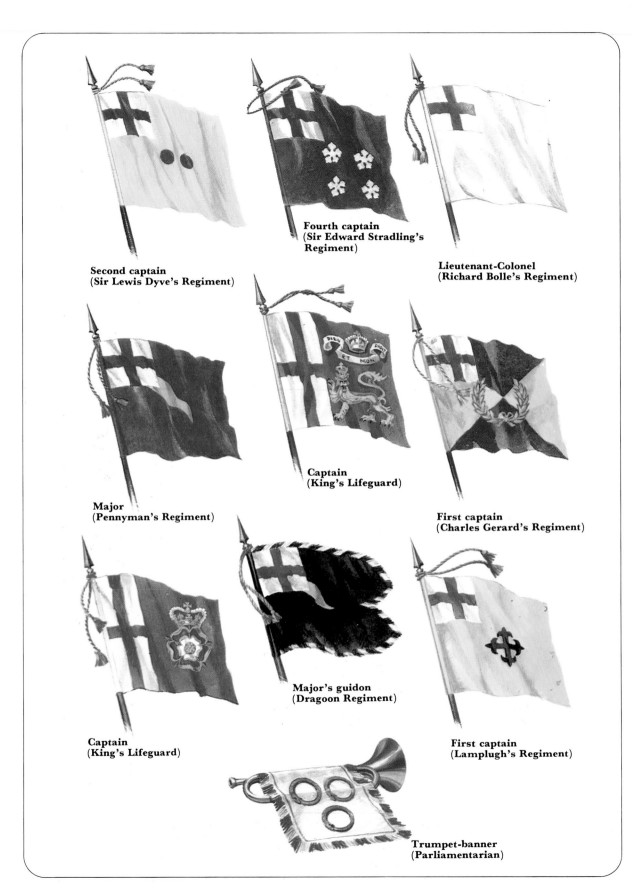

**Second captain
(Sir Lewis Dyve's Regiment)**

**Fourth captain
(Sir Edward Stradling's
Regiment)**

**Lieutenant-Colonel
(Richard Bolle's Regiment)**

**Major
(Pennyman's Regiment)**

**Captain
(King's Lifeguard)**

**First captain
(Charles Gerard's Regiment)**

**Captain
(King's Lifeguard)**

**Major's guidon
(Dragoon Regiment)**

**First captain
(Lamplugh's Regiment)**

**Trumpet-banner
(Parliamentarian)**

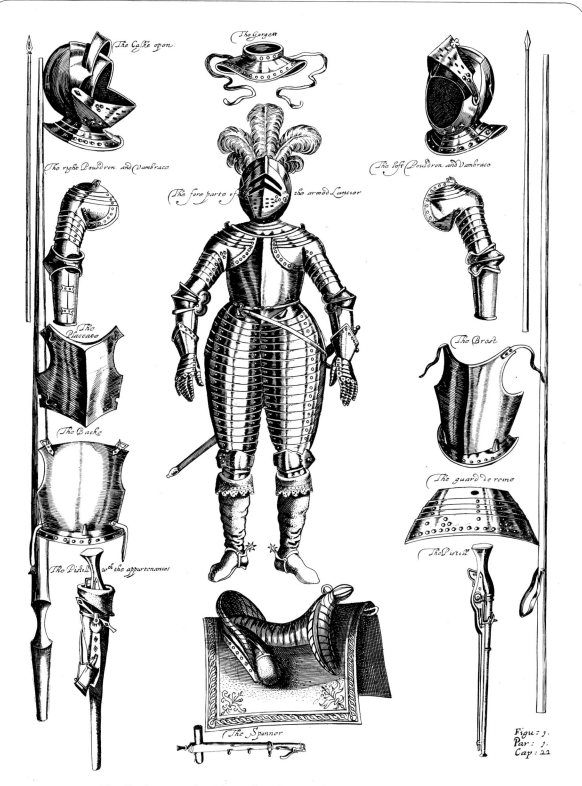

The Cafke open.

The Gorgett

The right Pouldron and Vambrace

The foft Pouldron and Vambrace

The fore parte of the armed Lancier

The Placcate

The Breft

The Backe

The guard de reine

The Piftoll wth the appurtenances

The Piftoll

The Spanner

Figu: 1.
Par: 1.
Cap: 22

The Equipment of a Heavy Cavalryman, from John Cruso's *Militarie Instructions for the Cavall'rie* (1632). **It is especially interesting to observe how very different the saddle is from the military saddle of modern times**

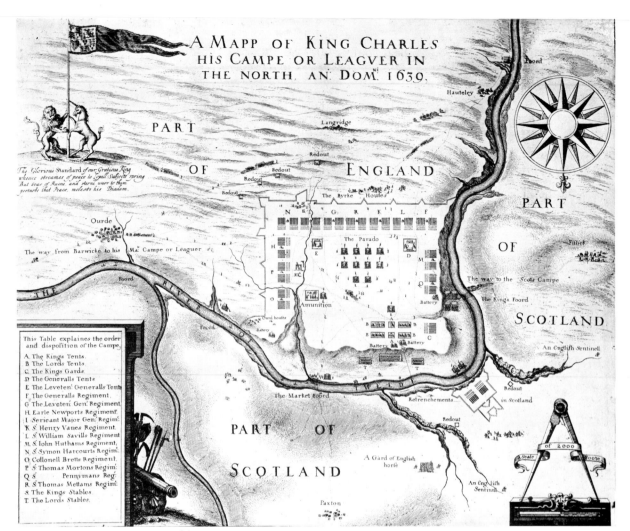

A MAPP OF KING CHARLES
HIS CAMPE OR LEAGVER IN
THE NORTH, AN: DOM: 1639.

The Glorious Standard of our Gratious King
whence streames of peace to Loyall Subjects springe
But Seas of Ruine and sterne warr to them
perturbe that Peace, molests his Diadem.

PART

OF

ENGLAND

The way from Barwicke to his Ma: Campe or Leaguer

THE RIVER TWEED

PART

OF

SCOTLAND

PART

OF

SCOTLAND

This Table explaines the order
and disposition of the Campe.

A. The Kings Tents.
B. The Lords Tents.
C. The Kings Gards.
D. The Generalls Tents.
E. The Leveten: Generalls Tent
F. The Generalls Regiment.
G. The Leveten: Gen: Regiment.
H. Earle Newports Regiment.
I. Serieant Major Gen: Regim:
K. S: Henry Vanes Regiment.
L. S: William Savills Regiment
M. S: Iohn Huthams Regiment,
N. S: Symon Harcourts Regim:
O. Collonell Bretts Regiment.
P. S: Thomas Mortons Regim:
Q. S: Pennymans Reg:
R. S: Thomas Mettams Regim:
S. The Kings Stables.
T. The Lords Stables.

King Charles's camp near Berwick during the First Scots War, 1639. The Glorious Standard is no doubt the same one raised at Nottingham when, in August 1642, the King declared war. Some of the colonels listed took part in the Civil Wars. The Earl of Newport was for a short time Lieutenant-General to the Earl of Newcastle, but quarrelled with him and was imprisoned in Pontefract Castle. Vane and Hotham were Roundheads. Savile had a regiment of redcoats in 1639, and it is likely that his regiment was re-raised for the King in 1642. Harcourt took his regiment to Ireland and was killed there. Jerome Brett became a sergeant-major-general. Sir William Pennyman's Yorkshire regiment was the first raised in 1642; he was Governor of Oxford and died there in 1643, and his regiment was eventually destroyed at Naseby. Old Sir Thomas Metham of Metham, Yorkshire (c. 1575–1644), commanded a troop of gentlemen volunteers, of which Newcastle himself was nominally the captain, and was killed at its head at Marston Moor

Captain Primrose had only 19 men and Captain Marford but 15. John Hampden, whose regiment did not arrive at Edgehill until the battle was over, still had 893 men on 21 January 1643. His numbers dwindled more gradually and by 21 June, when he was lying on his death-bed at Thame, he still had 849 men. Some may have been lost at the siege of Reading and elsewhere, but most had probably succumbed to the fevers so prevalent in the Thames Valley in the summer of 1643.

FORMATIONS

A body of foot normally marched in column of fours, but when it came to fight it was drawn up in a deeper formation. At Edgehill Essex had his men eight deep, which was the formation in the Dutch Army when he was a colonel there. The Royalists on that occasion were six deep, with their tertias arrayed in what was known as the 'Swedish brigade'. A regiment or body of foot normally fought with a solid hedgehog of pikes in the centre and with musketeers on the flanks. If cavalry threatened, the musketeers would take cover among the pikemen.

ARMS, DRESS AND EQUIPMENT

The appearance of the armies of 1642 would have pained the Duke of Cumberland, King George IV and Marshal Bernadotte; but, all the same, they did present some show of uniformity, as any unit will if they receive general issues of clothing, arms and equipment. At the time of the Civil Wars commissioned officers and even sergeants seem to have worn pretty much what they pleased, but the soldiers, particularly in the foot, were given such items as caps, coats, breeches, stockings and 'snapsacks', as well as their arms and armour. Unfortunately, we have no record of the coat colours of the majority of regiments engaged, but some are known.

Prince Maurice (1620–52). The favourite brother of Prince Rupert was a stout-hearted fighter. He was with his brother in several of his exploits – at Powick Bridge, Edgehill and Cirencester – before being given an independent command. He defeated Sir William Waller at Ripple (13 April 1643) and played a great part in the victories of the Western Army at Lansdown and Roundway Down. He took Exeter and Dartmouth, but failed to capture Plymouth and Lyme. He commanded the Western Army in the victories at Lostwithiel and at Second Newbury, where they were driven from Speen village. He was under Rupert at Naseby. When part of the fleet came over to the Royalists in 1648 Maurice served in it under his brother. He was lost at sea. His portrait by Dobson belongs to the Earl of Dartmouth

ROYALIST

The King's Lifeguard	Red
The Queen's Lifeguard	Red
Prince Charles C.O.: Sir Michael Woodhouse	Red (?)
The Duke of York C.O.: Sir William St Leger	Red (?)
(1) Sir Allen Apsley (2) Edward Hopton	Red
Lord Inchquin	Red
Sir William Savile	Red
Lord Hopton	Blue
(1) Sir Thomas Lunsford (2) Prince Rupert	Blue
Charles Gerard	Blue
Sir William Pennyman	Blue (?)
(1) Sir Ralph Dutton (2) (Sir) Stephen Hawkins	White
Marquis of Newcastle's Regiment	White
Lord Percy	White
(1) Thomas Pinchbeck (2) Sir Henry Bard	Grey
Sir Francis Gamul	Yellow (?)
(1) Sir Charles Vavasour (2) (Sir) Matthew Appleyard	Yellow
Sir John Paulet	Yellow
[?] Talbot	Yellow
Sir Thomas Blackwall	Black (?)
Robert Broughton	Green
Earl of Northampton	Green (?)
Henry Tillier	Green

PARLIAMENTARIAN

Denzil Holles	Red
Edward Montagu	Red lined white
Lord Robartes	Red
Sir Henry Cholmley	Blue
Sir William Constable	Blue
(1) Lord Saye and Sele (2) Sir John Meldrum (3) Edward Aldrich	Blue (?)
Earl of Stamford	Blue
Thomas Ballard	Grey
Sir John Merrick	Grey
John Hampden	Green
Earl of Manchester	Green lined red
Earl of Essex	Orange
Lord Brooke	Purple
Thomas Grantham	Russet (?)
Earl of Denbigh (Horse)	Grey (?)

A letter from Charles II when Prince of Wales commissioning Sir Edward Hopton of Canon Frome, Herefordshire, to be in command of a regiment of foot.

The Marquis of Newcastle's men are generally described as 'Whitecoats'. It seems that his army – not only his own regiment – wore coats of undyed woollen cloth. Percy's Whitecoats and Pinchbeck's Greycoats both came to Oxford from Newcastle's Army at the same time. It would seem that the dress of Newcastle's 'Lambs' was not exactly as white as snow.

Red was a fairly popular colour in the Cavalier Army, especially, it seems, in the Royal regiments. From the time of the formation of the New Model Army it was adopted by the Parliamentarians, from whom the Standing Army of King Charles II and his successors inherited it.

ARMS

When the war began there were not nearly enough arms to equip all the men who enlisted for the King. The armouries of the trained bands, as well as those of private individuals, were insufficient to provide weapons for all the volunteers. A number of those who fought at Edgehill had nothing better than some converted farm implement or a stout stave. Many of the weapons and pieces of armour had already seen service at the time of the Armada, or even maybe of Flodden and Bosworth. On the other hand, those were days when noblemen and gentlemen commonly had substantial armouries of their own. If the Royalist pikemen were short of corselets it was not really such a hardship: a steel helmet and a good buff coat would keep out many a savage blow, and, marching in body armour can have been no joke.

As for the Roundheads, they had at their command the great armouries of the Tower of London and of Hull. Their troops must have

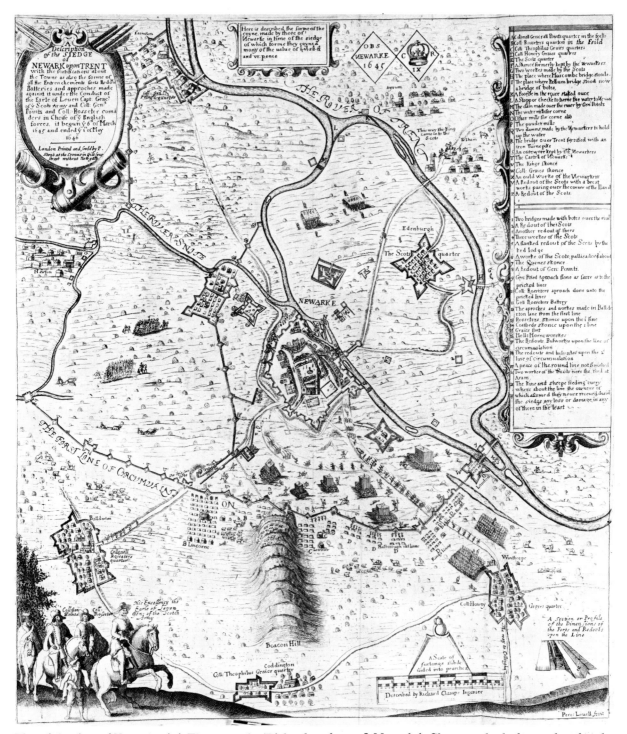

Plan of the siege of Newark, 1646. The survey by 'Richard Clampe Ingenier' was engraved by Peregrine Lovell, and printed and sold by Peter Stent at the sign of the Crown and later of the White Horse in Giltspur Street without Newgate. This plan was certainly on sale before 1650. The engraving, 20 inches by 17 inches, covers an area of about two miles radius around Newark and shows the works made for the last siege, which lasted from November 1645 to 8 May 1646. Clampe, who had served under the Earl of Manchester, and Sir Thomas Fairfax – presumably in the New Model – seems to have been the chief engineer of the Parliamentarian Army before Newark. He was rewarded in 1647 with the searcher's post at the port of King's Lynn in Norfolk. (Courtesy of the Royal Commission on Historical Monuments (England). Crown Copyright)

appeared armed very much according to the regulations of the day.

In theory, all ranks carried swords, those of the officers being no doubt of superior quality. With the exception of the ensign, who carried the company colour, the company officers were armed with partisans, while the sergeant's halbert was at once his weapon and his badge of rank. The pikemen had a weapon between sixteen and eighteen feet in length, and wore back-and-breast – the corselet – and a helmet. The musketeers had no body armour, but were generally equipped with a matchlock musket, and a bandolier. Some certainly had a rest, but this seems to have been obsolescent by the time of the Civil Wars. A few had the snaphance, or firelock, an early flintlock musket; but this was rare and was usually given to the escort of the train of artillery, for matchlocks and powder-barrels were unhappy partners. The bayonet was not yet to be seen among the English infantry.

The Train of Artillery

Artillery had proved its worth in battles as well as in sieges as early as the middle of the fifteenth century; it was as decisive at Castillon as at Constantinople. But its progress had been slow, and, at the time of the Civil Wars, many of its characteristics were still very unsatisfactory. Ranges were short, rates of fire slow, equipment heavy and means of traction uneconomical. Nevertheless, both round-shot and case-shot were damaging missiles, which could score heavily off a troop of horse or a stand of pikes, whilst for siege work the big guns were invaluable.

Clarendon describes the train of artillery as 'a spunge that can never be filled or satisfied', and it was only with the greatest difficulty that Sir John Heydon (d. 1653), the Royalist Lieutenant-General of the Ordnance, a noted mathematician and a thoroughly competent administrator, managed to put twenty guns in the field, six of them big ones. These guns were mostly made of brass. The trophies of Edgehill included seven guns and at First Newbury the Royalists had heavier metal.

At Naseby the King had only twelve big guns. Among those captured by the New Model Army were two demi-cannons, probably the same two that had been at Edgehill, and two mortars. Two of the great brass guns taken at Naseby were afterwards used by the Parliamentarians besieging Worcester.

The Roundheads, backed by the resources of the Tower of London, where since medieval times the Board of Ordnance had had its headquarters, were much better provided with guns than were their opponents. In the 1642 campaign they had over forty guns. Unfortunately for them their lieutenant-general, a foreigner named Philibert Emanuel du Boys, proved incapable of collecting a sufficient number of draught-horses, and many of the guns arrived too late for the battle of Edgehill. The train of artillery required a great deal of transport, for its ammunition and stores. A Royalist bye-train of four big guns detailed to attack Banbury Castle in October 1642 required the support of fifty-seven wagons.

The personnel – officers and specialists of various categories – was also very considerable. In 1642 Essex's Train had over 40 officers, 600 pioneers, besides 100 firelocks, to guard the train; engineers, commissaries, provost, gentlemen-of-the-ordnance, fireworkers, battery-master and bridge-master were all to be found in its ranks. The dress of artillerymen probably resembled that of the foot.

The supply of ammunition was not, it seems, very liberal. In the bye-train already referred to, the Royalists allowed fifty 'round shott of yron' per gun, and, in addition, twenty-four 'cases of tynn wth Muskett shott, or Cartouches'.

ROYALIST ORDNANCE

TYPES	EDGEHILL	NEWBURY	WEIGHT OF PIECE (lb)	LENGTH OF PIECE (ft)	WEIGHT OF SHOT (lb)
Demi-cannons	2	2	6,000	12	27
Culverins	2	2	4,000	11	15
Twelve-pounders	—	2	—	10–11	12
Demi-culverins	2	—	3,600	10	9
Six-pounders	—	5	—	—	6
Sakers	—	1	2,500	$9\frac{1}{2}$	$5\frac{1}{4}$
Mynions	—	2 (iron)	1,500	8	4
Three-pounders	—	4	—	—	3
Fawcons	6	—	700	6	$2\frac{1}{4}$
Fawconetts	6	—	210	4	$1\frac{1}{4}$
Rabonetts	2	—	120	3	$\frac{3}{4}$
Bases	—	2 (iron)	—	—	—
	20	20			

NOTES

1. This was Hopton's own troop.

2. Said to have been a son of Sir William Balfour, Lieutenant-General of the Horse in Essex's Army.

3. Cavalry at speed could cover such a distance in half a minute. Their opponents would hardly have time for more than one volley.

4. Four or six troops should have had between sixteen and twenty-four commissioned officers.

5. Doubtless the major of the King's Lifeguard of Foot, who became lieutenant-colonel and was knighted in 1645: Sir William Leighton.

The Plates

A1 King Charles I (1600–49) in 1644

From a painting by William Dobson (1610–46). This plate shows the King in his normal campaigning dress. Of course, he did not always wear this costume. At Edgehill he is described as wearing a black velvet coat lined with ermine, and a steel cap covered with velvet. In a print of

1644 by Wenceslas Hollar (1607–77) he is shown in full cuirassier's armour, of the sort worn by Sir Richard Willys (F3). Hollar was a Royalist soldier and served in the defence of Basing House. There can be little doubt, therefore, that he had actually seen the King thus armoured.

A2 Sir Edward Walker (1612–77)

Walker, who became Chester Herald in 1638, was with King Charles continuously from 1642 to 1645. He was at first Secretary at War (1642) and later Secretary of the Privy Council (1644). He was knighted in 1645. A number of his papers, dealing with military affairs are preserved in the British Museum, and his excellent accounts of the 1644 and 1645 campaigns are published in his *Historical Discourses* (London, 1705). At the Restoration Walker became Garter King-of-Arms. In this plate, which is taken from a painting by Dobson in the National Portrait Gallery, Walker wears the ordinary campaigning dress of a Cavalier gentleman, though without back- and breastplate.

A3 Prince Charles, later King Charles II (1630–85) in 1642

From the portrait by William Dobson in the Scottish National Portrait Gallery. The armour the Prince is wearing is still in existence in the armouries at the Tower of London. In this portrait Prince Charles is dressed as he was at the battle of Edgehill, 23 October 1643. On that occasion he was in danger of being captured when Sir William Balfour's Horse broke through the Royalist centre. Indeed he was seen winding up his wheel-lock pistols and crying out, 'I fear them not', before his escort of Gentlemen Pensioners hurried him from the field.

The Prince wears the normal costume of a cavalry officer of the day, a sleeveless buff coat with back-and-breast. In his hand he carries a baton, as a general did in those days. In 1645, when he was fifteen he was nominally in command of the West Country.

B Sir Charles Lucas (k. 1648)

Lucas was a professional soldier who had served in the Dutch Army. At Edgehill he was lieutenant-

---

Examples of Newark siege money. (Top) the face and obverse of a 1645 9d. piece; (bottom) face and obverse of a 1646 shilling. These lozenge-shaped coins were an emergency issue, probably authorized by the King himself. The main reason for their issue may have been the Governor's need to pay the townsmen for billeting the garrison.

Siege money was also issued at Carlisle, Chester and Pontefract Castle. The Newark coins of 1645 and 1646, ranging in value from 6d. to 2s. 6d., are among the best. They seem to have been made by slicing the lozenge-shaped blanks from rolled-out plates of silver, and then struck by some sort of mechanical hammer. This was probably a horse or water-operated trip hammer. The word OBS: on the reverse of the coins is the Latin *obsessum* — besieged

Back, breast and pot. These pieces of armour preserved at Broughton Castle were doubtless worn by a soldier serving under Lord Saye and Sele. The helmet is rather curious for it seems to be something between a burgonet and a morion

colonel in the Earl of Caernarvon's Regiment. He greatly distinguished himself by rallying 300 horse of the Royalist left wing and charging into the rear of the Roundhead foot. He was soon made colonel and early in 1644, through Rupert's influence, he became Lieutenant-General of the Horse in Newcastle's Army. Unfortunately, he was taken prisoner at Marston Moor. He was executed after the siege of Colchester in 1648. Lucas was an expert commander of horse, and wrote a treatise on the art of war. It was in cipher and so nobody could understand it; its whereabouts, too, are now unknown.

This plate is a reconstruction based on a portrait by Dobson in the National Portrait Gallery. Sir Charles is shown winding up his wheel-lock pistol.

C Trumpeter, Captain Sir Richard Astley's Troop of Horse

This figure is taken from Astley's monument in Patshull Church, in which the Captain, preceded by his two trumpeters is seen riding at the head of his troop. This trumpeter is dressed very much like those one sees fairly frequently in Dutch paintings of the period. His trumpet-banner, like the standard of the troop, and the Captain's holster-caps and saddle-cloth, bears the cinquefoil of Astley.

Sir Richard Astley, Bart. (1625–88) was the eldest son of Walter Astley, a Roman Catholic. He garrisoned Patshull House, near Wolverhampton, which was captured on 14 February 1645 by a Roundhead force from the garrison of Stafford. Astley was one of the garrison of Dudley Castle when it surrendered on 14 May 1646. He belonged to the small army under Lord Loughborough, the Royalist Lieutenant-General in the Midlands. There is some evidence that he fought in the 1651 campaign. Astley succeeded to his father's estates in 1654 and was made a baronet in 1662. A man of exemplary piety, he had one other claim to fame: an ingenious invention, whose details are not explained, for matching game-cocks.

John, first Baron Byron of Rochdale, K.B. (d. 1652) was Lieutenant of the Tower from December 1641 to February 1642. When he joined the King at York his regiment of horse was the first in the field. Byron was an unlucky soldier and a poor tactician, but he was brave and dogged. He played a great part in the victory at Roundway Down and distinguished himself at First Newbury. He was, however, severely defeated at Nantwich and Montgomery Castle. It was largely thanks to his faulty dispositions that Rupert's right wing was routed at Marston Moor. At the end of the war Byron, who had been made a baron in October 1643, clung on first to Chester and then to Caernarvon with the utmost resolution.

This portrait by William Dobson may well have been painted at Oxford in January 1643, for the scar on Byron's countenance is probably the halbert wound he received in a fight at Burford on the night of 1 January, as the Royalist weekly newspaper *Mercurius Aulicus* records

D Officer of Horse or Dragoons

This dashing character might belong to either side. He is an unashamed reconstruction based on a figure on the title-page of Cruso's *Instructions for the Cavall'rie* (1632) and a contemporary painting by a Dutch artist. The helmet is of the Dutch or German type. It was probably the exception rather than the rule for a dragoon to wear back-and-breast, for they were really mounted infantry, and usually fought on foot. It is true that Colonel John Okey's Regiment, belonging to the new Model, made a mounted charge into the Royalist foot at the end of the battle of Naseby; and one

also finds instances of men firing carbines or fowling-pieces from the saddle in a mêlée: Sir James Colborne's exploit at Babylon Hill is a case in point.

It was by no means unknown for mounted troops to be armed with a brace of pistols in addition to a carbine. Richard Symonds of the King's Lifeguard records a skirmish between Stilton and Huntingdon on 24 August 1645. The Roundheads, 400 strong, raised in Suffolk and Essex, were under Lieutenant-Colonel Lehunt. 'They a little disputed Huntingdon, but wee entered, notwithstanding a large ditch encompassed it. . . . Theise rebells ran away to Cambridge; all of them back and breast, headpeice, brace of pistoll, officers more. Every troope consisted of 100.'

While admitting that our plate is a reconstruction, it seems fair to assert that riders so equipped were to be seen in many an affair of the English Civil Wars.

E1 Pikeman, Lord Brooke's Regiment

Robert Greville, second Baron Brooke (1608–43) clothed his regiment of foot in purple. In this he seems to have been unique – just as well perhaps. The regiment was raised in London. It had purple colours with the usual cross of St George in all except the colonel's colour, and with the captain's ensigns differenced by a varying number of stars. The regiment, about 1,000 strong in September, lost heavily at Edgehill, and was down to 480 by mid-November. It suffered again at Brentford (12 November) and, it is thought, did not long survive the death of its colonel, sniped by 'Dumb' Dyott at the siege of Lichfield on 2 March 1643. Dyott fired from the tower of St Chad's Cathedral upon that saint's day. Royalists were not slow to point out the miraculous nature of this event.

E2 Roundhead Commander

This figure is based on a portrait reproduced in black and white in R. N. Dore's useful work *The Civil Wars in Cheshire*. The officer is thought to be Colonel John Booth. The instrument slung round his neck is a spanner such as was used in those days to wind up wheel-lock firearms. His beautiful carbine is probably an expensive fowling-piece. It was doubtless with such a weapon that Sir James Colborne was armed at Babylon Hill.

E3 Musketeer

This soldier is armed with a matchlock musket. He has made-up cartridges, 'The Twelve Apostles', hanging from his bandolier, a leather bag containing spare bullets, and a powder-flask. In his right hand he carries a rest to help him aim his heavy firearm. Rests do not seem to be mentioned ever in the Royalist ordnance papers that survive

Henry Ireton (1611–51). Educated at Trinity College, Oxford, and the Middle Temple, Ireton took up arms in 1642 and fought at Edgehill. Although he held high appointments he was no great soldier. He led the cavalry of the Roundhead left at Naseby, but was wounded and captured in the fighting. Rupert, though outnumbered, drove his men from the field. He married Cromwell's daughter, Bridget, and was his chief supporter during the trial of Charles I. He was one of the regicides who signed the death-warrant. Ireton went to Ireland as Cromwell's deputy and carried out his bloodthirsty policy with diligence and honesty. He died of a fever

in the Public Record Office. It may be that it was simply assumed that every musket had its rest just as it had its ramrod. On the other hand, it may be that this was a transition period and that the rest was going out. Of the four musketeers depicted in the Farndon Church window only two have rests.

John Lambert (1619–83). Lambert took up arms for Parliament in 1642, and by 1643 was commanding a regiment of horse in Yorkshire. He fought at Marston Moor, and in July 1647 superseded Poyntz in command of the Northern Forces. In 1648–49 he besieged Pontefract Castle, and in 1650 went to Scotland with Cromwell as major-general. He was wounded and captured at Musselburgh (30 July) but immediately rescued. He fought at Dunbar, and routed Sir John Brown at Inverkeithing, Fifeshire (20 July 1651). In the Worcester campaign he captured the important bridge at Upton-on-Severn, and at Worcester had his horse shot under him. He was the leader of the officers who offered the post of Protector to Cromwell, and was one of his council of state, but he broke with him over the question of a royal title. In 1660 he resisted Monck in vain and he ended his days in prison in Guernsey

F1 Lieutenant of a bluecoats regiment

The Royalist regiment of Colonel Charles Gerard, fought at Edgehill and First Newbury before going to South Wales when Gerard was put in command there early in 1644. There were bluecoats on either side and, except for the difference in the colour of sashes, it would have been easy to mistake a Roundhead officer of the Earl of Stamford's Regiment for one of Gerard's. Colonels Sir Henry Cholmley and Sir William Constable also commanded bluecoat regiments in the Earl of Essex's Army during the Edgehill Campaign of 1642.

On at least two occasions Royalist officers were captured through mistaking an enemy regiment for one of their own. This happened to Rupert's friend, Will Legge, at Southam (August 1642), when he mistook Hampden's men for the Earl of Northampton's, and to Lieutenant-Colonel Frank Butler at Nantwich (January 1644).

This officer carries a partisan, which was the

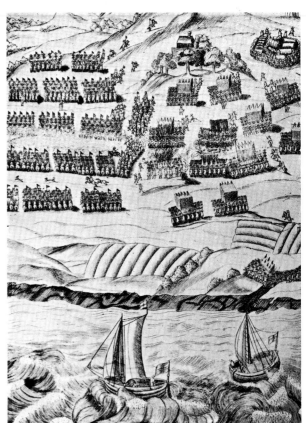

A detail from a contemporary engraving of the battle of Dunbar, 3 September 1650. This plan, which is preserved in the Bodleian Library, was made by Payne Fisher, who was educated at Hart Hall, Oxford, and Magdalene College, Cambridge. He served in the Netherlands, against the Scots, in Ireland, and fought for the King at Marston Moor. He then abandoned the Royalist cause and in 1652 went to Scotland as an official historian.

Sir Charles Firth, who discovered this plan, identified the building surrounded by trees in the background as Meikle Pinkerton farmhouse. The bodies of foot ranged in front of it on the hillside, below it are Scots. A few Scots cavalrymen may be seen breaking away and fleeing up Doon Hill as the Cromwellian cavalry attack develops in the left foreground. The Scots under David Leslie outnumbered the English by two to one, but they made a tactical error by leaving the high ground, and Cromwell was able to score one of his most brilliant successes

Colonel Richard Grace (1621?–91). A Roman Catholic son of Robert Grace, Baron of Courtown, he distinguished himself in the First Civil War in Prince Rupert's Regiment of Horse, and fought at Marston Moor. As a captain he was taken prisoner soon after at Welshpool when the regiment was beaten up in its quarters at night (22 June 1644). He was with the garrison of Oxford in March 1645 and took part in Colonel Will Legge's raid on Headington in June. He commanded Ormonde's Regiment in the Royalist Army at the battle of Dunkirk Dunes in 1658, and managed to retreat in good order. In 1691 he was Governor of Athlone where he died fighting for King James II

weapon, and indeed the badge, of captains and, lieutenants, though the former were entitled to have them with gilded heads. In practice, one imagines, the blades were probably of plain steel.

F2 Colonel Nathaniel Fiennes (1608?–69)

From a painting by Mirevelt belonging to Lord Saye and Sele at Broughton Castle, Oxfordshire. In 1642 Fiennes, who was M.P. for Banbury, was captain of a troop of horse in Essex's Army. Routed at Powick Bridge (23 September 1642), at Edgehill his men did better for they were with Sir William Balfour whose charges broke the brigades of Colonel Richard Feilding and Sir Nicholas Byron. Promoted colonel he was unjustly disgraced after the fall of Bristol (26 July 1643), and had it not been for the intervention of the Earl of Essex might have been condemned to death. Though excluded from the House of Commons by Pride's Purge (1648), he sat in Cromwell's House of Lords (1658). Nathaniel Fiennes was the second son of the first Viscount Saye and Sele.

Points to note in this plate are the steel gauntlet which protects his bridle-arm, and the fact that his armour has been painted black to prevent rust. His helmet looks like a continental one, though he had never served abroad. Although he was a cavalryman, his breastplate with its short tassets looks rather like that of an officer of pikemen. His scarf is typical of those worn by the Roundheads; orange-tawny being the colours of the Earl of Essex.

F3 Colonel Sir Richard Willys (1614–90)

This plate is taken from a half-length portrait by Dobson, which belongs to Newark Corporation, and – as to the legs – from the monument to Edward St John, 'The Golden Cavalier', in the church at Lydiard Tregoze, Wiltshire. Willys is fully equipped as a cuirassier. The whole of Sir Arthur Hesilrige's Regiment of Horse on the Parliament side were armoured in this fashion, and so in 1642 were Essex's Lifeguard. On the Royalist side individuals fitted themselves out in this style. The Earl of Northampton, K.B. (1601–43) was wearing full armour when he was killed at Hopton Heath (19 March 1643). Several suits belonging to the Popham family (Parliamentarian) are still to be seen at Littlecote House near Hungerford, a place which is well worth a visit.

One pities the horse that had to carry men dressed in this fashion; it was also not particularly convenient for the man himself. Edmund Ludlow (Essex's Lifeguard) was dismounted at Edgehill

and writes, 'I could not without great difficulty recover on horse-back again [remount], being loaded with cuirassier's arms, as the rest of the guard also were.' During the night after the battle he was starving, 'neither could I find my servant who had my cloak, so that having nothing to keep me warm but a suite of iron, I was obliged to walk about all night, which proved very cold by reason of a sharp frost'.

Sir Richard Willys of Fen Ditton, Cambridgeshire, distinguished himself as an ensign of foot in the Dutch Army at the siege of Breda (1637). In 1640 he was major to Goring's Regiment of Foot in the Scots War. During the next two years he served in King Charles's guard at Whitehall and at Hampton Court. Willys was knighted on

Colonel Sir John Gell's buff coat, from a photograph taken in 1965. The coat has come down in the family to Colonel Chandos-Pole, and must be one of very few whose original owner can be positively identified. Sir John Gell, Bart. (1583–1671), was the Parliamentarian leader in Derbyshire. He and his men were notorious for their love of plunder. After Naseby he was suspected of conniving at the escape of Royalist prisoners, and in 1650 he was imprisoned and fined for plotting against the Commonwealth. He supported the Restoration

A Royalist officer from the stained glass window in the Barnston Chapel in Farndon Church, Cheshire. This is Captain William Barnston of Churton (d. 1664) who served in Colonel Sir Francis Gamul's Regiment during the defence of Chester. It may have been the City Trained Band Regiment. The Captain-Lieutenant of the regiment was Richard Barnston, perhaps a younger brother, of William; he was alive at the Restoration for he is in

A List of [Indigent] Officers, 1663.
Captain Barnston carries a partisan in his hand, an indication of his rank. He also wears a gorget which shows that he is on duty. The uniform of this regiment seems to have been of a saffron shade of yellow, with the officers wearing buff coats. Other windows from Farndon Church are shown above and on the facing page

1 October 1642 and served as major of Lord Grandison's Regiment of Horse at Edgehill. Taken prisoner at Winchester in December he escaped and was commissioned as colonel of horse on 8 February 1643. In April he was Sergeant-Major-General of Horse in Lord Capel's Army operating in the Shrewsbury and Chester area. He was captured again at Ellesmere, Shropshire, on 11 January 1644, but was exchanged, and by 11 October was back at Oxford. He was *persona grata* with Prince Rupert and was promoted Colonel-General of the forces in Nottinghamshire,

Lincolnshire and Rutland. He had his headquarters at Newark and was Governor there until replaced by Belasyse in October 1645, because he had supported Prince Rupert in the quarrels that followed his surrender of Bristol.

In 1653 Willys became a member of the 'Sealed Knot', the committee which tried to co-ordinate Royalist opposition to the Commonwealth. It is thought that he kept Cromwell's secretary, John Thurloe, informed of its activities. Though not employed after the Restoration he does not appear to have been punished.

G1 Ensign, Lamplugh's Regiment of Foot

Colonel John Lamplugh of Lamplugh was wounded and captured at Marston Moor. He commanded one of the regiments of the Northern Royalist Army, which were almost all dressed in white or grey, and were known as 'Newcastle's Whitecoats'. This particular regiment was raised in Cumberland and in Yorkshire. The colour shown, that of the first captain's company, was among those taken at Marston Moor, and shows a black cross *patonce* on a yellow field, as well as the cross of St George in the upper canton. The latter emblem was commonly used in practically all infantry colours in English armies, both Roundhead and Royalist, at this period. It is the single cross that shows that the colour belonged to the first captain's company. Yellow (gold) in a colour, according to Gervase Markham (*The Souldiers Accidence*, 1625), indicated honour, or height of spirit.

G2 Drummer of a redcoat regiment

At least as early as 1588 we find drummers' coats adorned with a quantity of gold or silver lace. Some Norwich accounts of that period describe them as being embellished with eleven yards of lace and six yards of pointing. In the eighteenth century drummers of the British Army usually wore coats of the colour of the regimental facings. Thus the drummers of the 16th Foot had yellow coats and those of the 50th had black. In the Civil Wars we sometimes find coats lined with a different colour, but 'facings' had not yet been invented. So when we learn that in October 1643 the Earl of Manchester ordered coats of 'green cloth lined with red' for his regiment in the Eastern Association, we must not assume that his drummers wore red coats. It is much more likely that they wore green, embellished with gold or silver lace. We have no reliable contemporary picture of a drummer of the Civil Wars since the example in the church window at Farndon, Cheshire, is copied from a picture belonging to the Gardes Françaises. The drum in our plate is reconstructed from the one shown serving as a table in Dobson's painting (1644) of King Charles dictating to Sir Edward Walker. It may safely be assumed that it belonged to the Lifeguard of Foot.

G3 Royalist Sergeant of a greencoat regiment

The Royalist regiments of Colonel Henry Tillier and Robert Broughton were raised during the Second Scots War, probably in 1640, and were sent to Ireland in 1642. In 1643 there was a cessation of hostilities in Ireland and these two regiments of greencoats were among about a dozen which were sent to Chester or to Bristol to reinforce the Royalist armies. Tillier's and Broughton's landed, 2,000 strong, in Cheshire on 7 February 1644. They were well-officered and experienced units, but there was a good deal of desertion from among the private soldiers. These two units were the backbone of the infantry of Prince Rupert's Army at the relief of Newark (21 March 1644). They suffered heavily at Marston Moor, where Major-General Tillier, a

In the Scots War Colonel Sir Bernard Astley (k. 1645) was major in his father's regiment of foot, and in 1643 he was Lieutenant-Colonel of the Marquis of Hertford's Regiment in the West. Hopton would have made him Sergeant-Major-General had he not fallen ill in the autumn of 1643. He commanded a brigade in the 1644 campaign and was killed during the siege of Bristol on 4 September 1645

dressed better than the common soldiers. In September 1642 the Roundhead Nehemiah Wharton had 'my mistress' scarf and Mr Molloyne's hatband . . . and had this day made me a soldier's sute for winter, edged with gold and silver lace'.

H Colours
All except the trumpet-banner are Royalist.

1st row

Second captain	Sir Lewis Dyve's Regiment; noted by Richard Symonds in April 1644.
Fourth captain	Sir Edward Stradling's Regiment; taken at Edgehill.
Lieutenant-Colonel	Richard Bolle's later George Lisle's Regiment; noted by Symonds in April 1644.

2nd row

Major	Pennyman's Regiment.
Captain	The King's Lifeguard.
First captain	Charles Gerard's Regiment; noted by Symonds in April 1644.

3rd row

Captain	The King's Lifeguard.
Major's guidon	Dragoon Regiment; taken at Marston Moor.
Trumpet-banner	Parliamentarian; taken at Cropredy Bridge.
First captain	Lamplugh's Regiment.

very stout and able soldier, was captured, but survived to fight at Montgomery Castle, and Naseby, by which time only a handful survived. The sergeant's halbert is his badge of rank. It was probably about eight feet in length. Sergeants

INDEX

GLOSSARY

ambuscade an ambush or trap

breastwork defensive wall

budge barrel small barrel for gunpowder (p6)

case shot smaller missiles encased in a container to be fired from a cannon

carbine a short rifle or musket (p6)

cashier to dismiss someone from a position of responsibility (p16)

cornet a pennant or standard, and thus also the officer who carried it (p17)

corselet body armour (p6)

cuirassier armoured horseman (pp22, 25)

dragoons mounted infantry, probably armed with carbines (p9, plate D)

ensign a colour or flag, and thus also the officer who carried it

field-piece a field gun, artillery

firelock a early flintlock musket (p6)

foot footsoldiers, infantry

galloper messenger

gantelope running the gauntlet (p18)

grape shot a cannon charge consisting of a large number of small missiles, an anti-personnel weapon (p6)

harquebusiers cavalry armed with guns (p22)

hedgehog fighting formation used by pikemen (pp6, 27)

horse mounted soldiers, cavalry and dragoons

linstock a staff with a forked end to carry match to set off cannon (p6)

matchlock firing device for a personal firearm, using a burning fuse (p6)

mêlée confused, usually hand-to-hand, fight

musket a long handgun (p6, plate E)

ordinance a law or proclamation

ordnance artillery

pike, pikemen a weapon with a blade mounted on a long shaft; men drilled to fight with the pike (p6, plate E)

pillory a device for public punishment which secured the standing victim by the neck and hands

push of pike distance between soldiers small enough to make use of the pike possible (p9)

renegade, renegadoe a person who changes sides

round shot a solid cannon-ball

sconce a castle or fort (pp19, 20)

skirmish fight between small numbers of troops (p9)

snap a snack, a meal eaten quickly

snaphance an early flintlock musket (p6)

snapsack a haversack to carry one's snap

standard a personal flag (pp9, 17, plate H)

stocks a device for public punishment which secured the seated victim by the ankles

tertia an organisational grouping of military units, a brigade, usually of three regiments (p24)

touch-hole hole through which gunpowder in a cannon is ignited

train a grouping of artillery on the move, including support and supply wagons

trained bands local militia troops (p24)

wheel-lock a mechanism for igniting the powder in a handgun (plate B).

SELECTED PLACES OF INTEREST

Opening times for museums and other buildings can change, so telephone numbers are given to allow readers to check. Battlefields are not described as space does not permit, but locations of important ones are given and useful books are listed in the reference section.

Central England

The Battle of Cropredy Bridge, 29 June 1644. Cropredy, four miles north of Banbury by A423 or A361 and minor roads. Parking near bridge over canal.

The Battle of Edgehill, 23 October 1642. Radway (Castle Inn viewpoint), seven miles north-west of Banbury by A422 and minor road to north.

The Battle of Naseby, 14 June 1645. Ten miles east of Rugby. The minor road north from Naseby village to Sibbertoft crosses the A14 and the monument and viewing table are in a field on the left, the west. There is a lay-by for three cars on the roadside at the start of the footpath.

The Museum of Oxford St Aldates, Oxford. Tel: (01865) 815559. Open Tuesday to Friday 10am to 4pm, Saturday 10am to 5pm.

The museum is devoted to the history of the city and of the university, but has some coverage of the Civil War, during which Oxford was Charles I's capital, including the map of de Gomme's fortifications and Cromwell's death mask. The Royalist Parliaments met in Christ Church Hall nearby.

The Battle of Chalgrove Field, 18 June 1643. Chalgrove, six miles south-east of Oxford by B480 on minor road to Warpsgrove. Here John Hampden was fatally wounded.

The Battle of Stow-on-the-Wold, 21 March 1646. Donnington, between the A424 and A429 north of Stow-on-the-Wold.

Newark-on-Trent Tourist information (Castlegate, Tel: 01636 78962) for details of the Governor's House and the Millgate Museum. The Queen's Sconce is at Devon Park, south-west of the town off the A46.

The Battle of Hopton Heath, 19 March 1643. Hopton, two miles north-east of Stafford by B5066 or A518 and minor roads.

The Battle of Winceby, 11 October 1643. Four miles east of Horncastle, Lincs, on B1195 Spilsby road, just south of junction with A158.

Southern England

The National Army Museum, Royal Hospital Road, Chelsea, London. Tel: (020) 7730 0717. Open daily 10am to 5.30pm. Underground station: Sloane Square.

The history of the British Army from the raising of the Yeoman of the Guard in 1485 to the present day is the subject of the museum. The Victorian Soldier Gallery tells the story of the British soldier from the Battle of Waterloo to the outbreak of World War I.

The National Maritime Museum, Romney Road, Greenwich.
Tel: (020) 8312 6565 (24 hour), (020) 8858 4422 (switchboard).
Open daily 10am to 5pm. Rail station: Greenwich or Maze Hill.
Pleasure boat from Westminster, Charing Cross or Tower Pier. Foot tunnel under river from Island Gardens.
The collection of the museum is vast and it is as well to plan your route to take in exactly what you want to see. The coverage is from the prehistoric to the present day. The English Civil War coverage makes use of the portraits in the Queen's House. By appointment with the Librarian the extensive collection of naval records, books, ships plans and manuscripts can be used.

The Battle of Brentford, 12 November 1642, High Street, Brentford, Middlesex and Syon Park. Rail station: Brentford Central.

West Gate Museum, St Peter's Street, Canterbury.
Tel: (01227) 452747. Open Monday to Saturday.
The towers of the gatehouse, built in 1380, are the earliest fortifications in England designed for guns. The keyhole gun-ports give overlapping fields of fire. The museum contains arms and armour from the Civil War, as well as the Boer War and World War II.

Farnham Castle, Farnham, Surrey, north of town centre on A287.
English Heritage. Tel: (01252) 713393. Open daily April
to September.
The original castle was built by Henry of Blois, Bishop of Winchester, in about 1138. The castle was stormed and taken by Sir William Waller for Parliament in 1642.

Newbury District Museum, The Wharf, Newbury.
Tel: (01635) 30511. Open April to September daily except
Wednesdays, 10am to 5pm and Sundays and Bank Holidays 1pm
to 5pm. October to March daily except Wednesdays and Sundays,
10am to 4pm.
The museum had a variety of displays on local matters and also extensive coverage of the Civil War including an audio-visual display featuring the two battles of Newbury.

The First Battle of Newbury, 20 September 1643. Between the A34 bypass and the A343 Andover road.

The Second Battle of Newbury, 27 October 1644 Donnington Castle, one mile north of Newbury by B4494. The castle is in the care of English Heritage; open site, exterior only to view.

Basing House, Redbridge Lane, Basing, two miles north-east of Basingstoke by minor road. Open April-September, Wednesday to Sunday & Bank Holidays.
The early Norman castle had been extensively modified before it saw real action in the Civil War. A Royalist stronghold, it was the southernmost of the strategically important north/south line through Donnington Castle, Oxford and Banbury. The ruins include the extensive earthworks that repulsed Sir William Waller in 1643 and were eventually overcome in October 1645, when the house was destroyed and the defenders slaughtered.

The Battle of Cheriton, 29 March 1644. Seven miles east of Winchester, south of New Alresford on B3046 and north of A272.

Carisbrooke Castle, south of Newport, Isle of Wight. English Heritage.
Tel: (01983) 522107. Open daily.
The first fortification here was built by the Romans and adapted by the Saxons in the 8th century. Improvements were made continuously for hundreds of years, making this a prime example of the evolution of the English castle. Carisbrooke was a prison to Charles I before his execution and his story forms part of the exhibition to be seen here.

The Battle of Roundway Down, 13 July 1643. Three miles north of Devizes by A361 and left on minor road to Calne.

Western England

The Battle of Lansdown Hill, 5 July 1643. Four miles north of Bath and north of the racecourse where the minor road drops steeply. On the Cotswold Way long distance path.

Admiral Blake Museum, Blake Street, Bridgwater, Somerset.
Tel: (01278) 456127. Open Tuesday to Saturday, 10am to 4pm.
Admiral Robert Blake, General-at-Sea under Cromwell's Protect-orate is reputed to have been born in this house in 1598. The museum contains personal memorabilia of the great admiral as well as a diorama of the Battle of Santa Cruz, one of his greatest victories. There are also displays on the Monmouth Rebellion and the Battle of Sedgemoor and the Civil War siege of Bridgwater.

The Battle of Langport, 10 July 1646. Langport, 20 miles east of Taunton by A358, A378 and B3153 to Somerton. The battle took place a short way along the Somerton road around the bridge over Wagg Rhyne

Bude-Stratton Museum, The Castle, Bude, Cornwall.
Tel: (01288) 353576.
Archive material includes coverage of the Battle of Stamford Hill or Stratton, a Civil War engagement.

The Battle of Stratton, 16 May 1643. Stamford Hill, Stratton, two miles east of Bude.

The Battle of Lostwithiel, 21 August – 2 September 1644. Beacon Hill, off the A390 just east of Lostwithiel, Cornwall, and Castle Dore, near the Golant turning on the B3269 to Fowey.

The Battle of Braddock Down, 19 January 1643. From Lostwithiel, three miles east by A390 and minor road through Trewindle towards Boconnoc.

Eastern England

Cromwell Museum, Grammar School Walk, High Street, Huntingdon.
Tel: (01480) 425830. Open April to October Tuesday to Friday 11am to 1pm and 2pm to 5pm, weekends the same closing 4pm; November to March the same, but closing 4pm and Sunday morning.
Oliver Cromwell was born in Huntingdon in 1599 and went to school in this building. The museum is devoted to the life of Cromwell and the Parliamentary side in the Civil War. There are portraits of the leading figures of the time and various of Cromwell's possessions including a surgeon's chest made by Kolb of Augsburg. The exhibits also include coins and medals.

Norris Museum, The Broadway, St Ives. Tel: (01480) 465101.
Open: Monday to Saturday 10am to 1pm and 2pm 5pm; closes earlier in winter.
The museum of Huntingdonshire, it deals with the broad history of the county but also includes special displays on the Civil War.

The Bulwark, Earith, 10 miles east of Huntingdon by A1123. Conditions of access not known; do not trespass.

To guard Ely from a Royalist advance from the west in the Civil War, Parliamentarian forces built a fort at Earith, between the New and the Old Bedford Rivers. The square earthwork has angle bastions at each corner and a covered way and a glacis, a sloping parapet, beyond the ditch.

Oliver Cromwell's House, 29 St Mary's Street, Ely. Tel: (01353) 662062. Open: daily 10am to 6pm; closes 5.15pm and Sunday October to March.

This was the family home of Oliver Cromwell, Lord Protector of England, and the museum deals not only with the man himself but also with the broader context of 17th century life.

Northern England

The Royal Armouries, The Waterfront, Leeds. Tel: 0990 106666 or 0113 245 6456. Open April to August 10am to 5pm, 6pm at weekends and in school holidays, September to March until 4pm, 5pm weekends.

The Battle of Adwalton Moor, 30 June 1643. Drighlington, nine miles south-west of Leeds by A58, on open land crossed by A650 east of Birkenshaw and north of Adwalton.

The Battle of Selby, 10 April 1644. Dam Fields or War Memorial Fields, near the Abbey, Selby.

York Castle Museum, next to Clifford's Tower, York. Tel: (01904) 653611. Open April to October Monday to Saturday 9.30am to 5.30pm, Sundays 10am to 5.30pm. November to March closes 4pm.

This fascinating museum of everyday life includes a military gallery with medieval and Civil War weapons; armour, swords, pole-arms and firearms. It also houses the Thornley Collection of orders and decorations.

The Battle of Marston Moor, 2 July 1644. Long Marston, seven miles west of York by B1224 and minor road to Tockwith.

Wales and the Marches

Llancaiach Fawr Living History Museum, Gelligaer Road (B4254), Nelson, seven miles north of Caerphilly by A469 via Ystrad Mynach and A472. Tel: (01443) 412248. Open daily, October to March afternoons on Sundays.

An opportunity to experience life in a Civil War stronghold. The scene is set in 1645 and visitors can use the furniture, try on clothes and take a turn in the stocks. Charles I visited the house on 5 August 1645.

Chepstow Castle, Chepstow. From Junction 22 of M4, via A466. Tel: (01291) 624065. C A D W. Open daily (Sunday afternoons in winter).

Here a rocky ridge offered the opportunity to use a promontory for defence and the stone tower raised in 1071 still stands. The castle was besieged in the Civil War as an exhibition records, and modified for cannon and musketry afterwards, remaining a military installation until 1690.

Raglan Castle, Raglan, 7 miles SW of Monmouth by A40. Tel: (01291) 690228. C A D W. Open daily, Sunday afternoons only in winter.

During the Civil War Raglan was besieged by Fairfax for 13 weeks and the great tower withstood artillery bombardment until it was taken at last on 19 August 1646 once it had been rendered useless by the undermining of its walls, leaving the shell we see today.

The Commandery Civil War Centre, Sidbury (leads from Cathedral to London Road A44), Worcester. Tel: (01905) 355071. Open daily, Sundays afternoon only.

The Commandery was Charles II's headquarters during the Battle of Worcester and now contains a museum dedicated to the Civil War. The London road was protected by an earthwork just outside the city walls and known here as Fort Royal.

The Battle of Worcester, 3 September 1651. Viewpoint off the A422 southern link road at the A38. Ketch Inn overlooks junction of the rivers Teme and Severn.

The Battle of Powick Bridge, 23 September 1642. West of the modern crossing of the River Teme by the A449 to Powick, south of Worcester, the old bridge survives.

Phoenix Tower or King Charles's Tower, Chester.
Charles I witnessed the defeat of his army at Rowton Heath from this tower and an exhibition in it presents the story.

The Battle of Rowton Heath, 24 September 1645. Rowton, four miles south-east of Chester by the A41.

The Battle of Nantwich, 25 January 1644. Acton, north-west of Nantwich which is 16 miles south-east of Chester. A canal-side path runs north from the marina to Henhull Bridge.

Scotland

The Battle of Auldearn, 9 May 1645. Two miles east of Nairn, which is 16 miles east of Inverness, on the A96. Follow the National Trust for Scotland signs to Boath Doocot viewpoint.

The Battle of Alford, 2 July 1646. Twenty-seven miles north-west of Aberdeen by A944 at the junction with the A980.

The Battle of Kilsyth, 15 August 1645. East of Kilsyth, which is 14 miles north-east of Glasgow, by A803 at Colzium-Lennox Park. Walk around the lake which covers part of the battlefield.

The Battle of Philiphaugh, 18 September 1645. Two miles west of Selkirk on the A708.

The Battle of Dunbar, 4 September 1650. Two miles south-east of Dunbar, near Broxburn.

SOCIETIES

Sealed Knot Society P O Box 2000, Nottingham, NG2 5LH. Email: sealed_knot@compuserve.com

English Civil War Society 70 Hailgate, Howden, East Riding of Yorkshire DN14 7ST. Email: ecws@jpbooks.com

REFERENCES

Baker, Anthony, *A Battlefield Atlas of the English Civil War*, Ian Allen, 1986.

Marix Evans, Martin, *The Military Heritage of Britain and Ireland*, André Deutsch, 1998.

Seymour, William, *Battles in Britain*, Wordsworth, 1997.

Smurthwaite, David, *The Complete Guide to the Battlefields of Britain*, Michael Joseph, 1993.